Chuck and Jack Luchsinger's

Cartoon
TeleTales

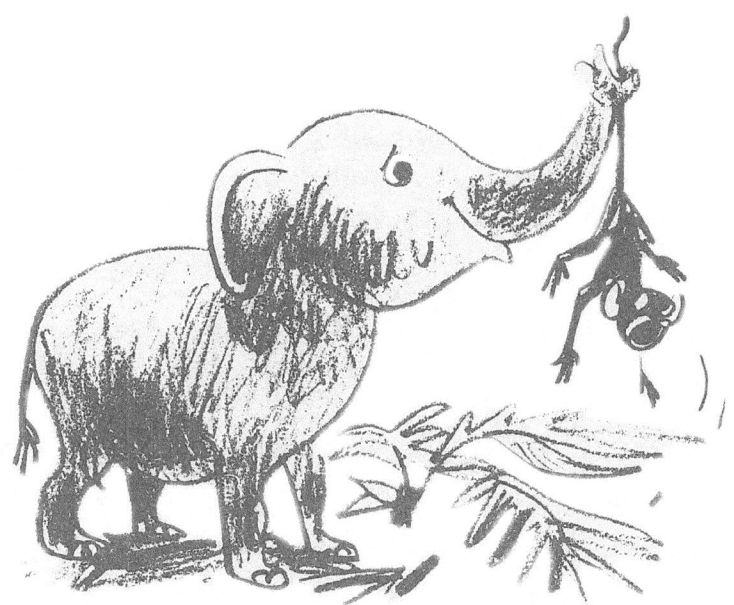

Written by Kevin Scott Collier

Chuck and Jack Luchsinger's
Cartoon TeleTales

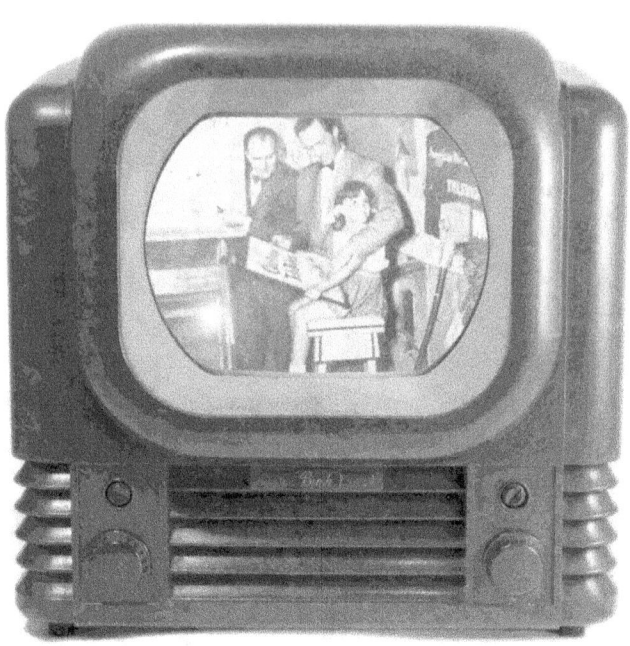

Written By
Kevin Scott Collier

CARTOON TELETALES, JOLLY GENE AND HIS FUN MACHINE and all related characters ©1948-1980 Chuck and Jack Luchsinger and the Luchsinger family.

All prominent characters mentioned in this book and the distinctive likenesses thereof are copywriter trademarks and properties of The Luchsinger Family, except where not indicated. The images included in this book are © their respective copyright holders and are used as Fair Use to be illustrative for the text contained herein.

CHUCK AND JACK LUCHSINGER'S CARTOON TELETALES is written and compiled by Kevin Scott Collier. Sources: The Luchsinger family, 1948-54 entertainment periodicals, promotional documents from the series, Library of Congress archives and misc.

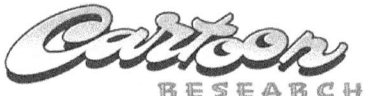

827 North Hollywood Way #100
Burbank, California 91505
Visit us online: www.cartoonresearch.com
Founder: Jerry Beck
Email: jerrybeck18@gmail.com

THIS BOOK IS DEDICATED TO THE LUCHSINGER FAMILY

A special thanks to Bob, Jay and Sandra Luchsinger, and the Luchsinger family for information, photographs, and access to a private video of a *Cartoon TeleTales* kinescope recording.

CHAPTER ONE
About Chuck and Jack Luchsinger

Brothers Chuck and Jack Luchsinger earn the distinction of creating and starring in the first network "cartoon" television series. While the show featured no animation, the two live-action siblings were animated enough to please a fast-growing audience of children.

The formula of their series, *Cartoon Tele-Tales*, was quite simple. It was to engage young imaginations to participate on many levels. "Moppets," as the juvenile viewers were called, learned to draw via Chuck Luchsinger's example, and inspire kids to unleash their own creativity.

The notion of combining artistic instruction with creative characters and stories established a fun formula for learning, raising the rousing approval of parents.

The pathway leading to the pioneering television program originated in childhood for the siblings.

Brothers Chuck and Jack Luchsinger were born and raised in Moline, Illinois. Their father, Jacob C. Luchsinger, provided for the family working as a machinist for a railroad shop, then later as a toolmaker at the John Deere Harvester Works factory, the leading employer in Moline.

Jacob and his wife, Florence Anna (Carlson) Luchsinger, both born in Illinois, had two other children, Velma and Richard. The children, including Jack and Chuck attended public schools, graduating from John Deere High School.

Charles (Chuck) Robert Luchsinger, born

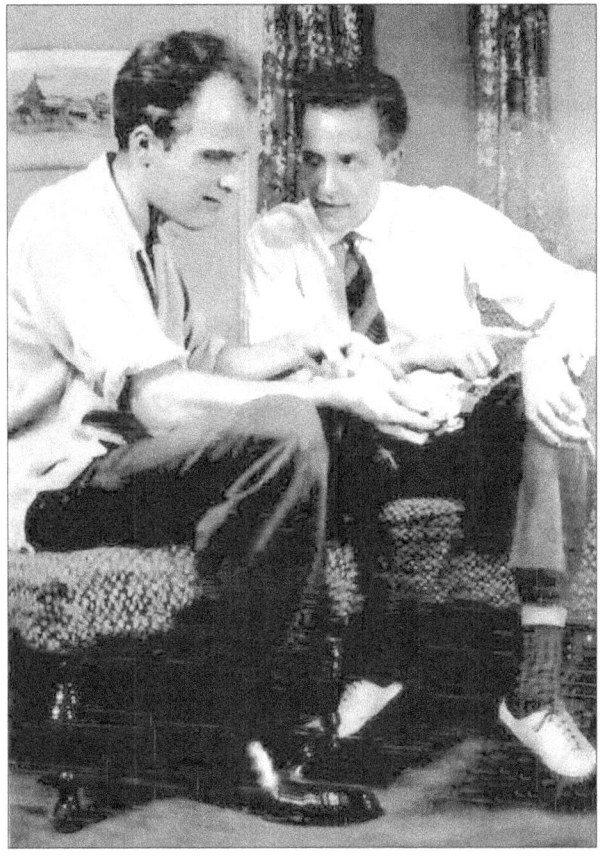

Chuck Luchsinger, left, and his brother Jack, right, 1940.

September 5, 1914, decided at the age of 6 he wanted to be a cartoonist. On his pathway to professional illustration, Luchsinger worked as a caddy, bellhop, elevator operator, ice man, gasoline station attendant, drill press operator, sign painter, and cartographer.

He also sold groceries, household appliances, and magazine subscriptions, then eventually working at an advertising agency.

Luchsinger shelled about $400 to attend the Art Institute of Chicago, where he studied drawing and painting.

3

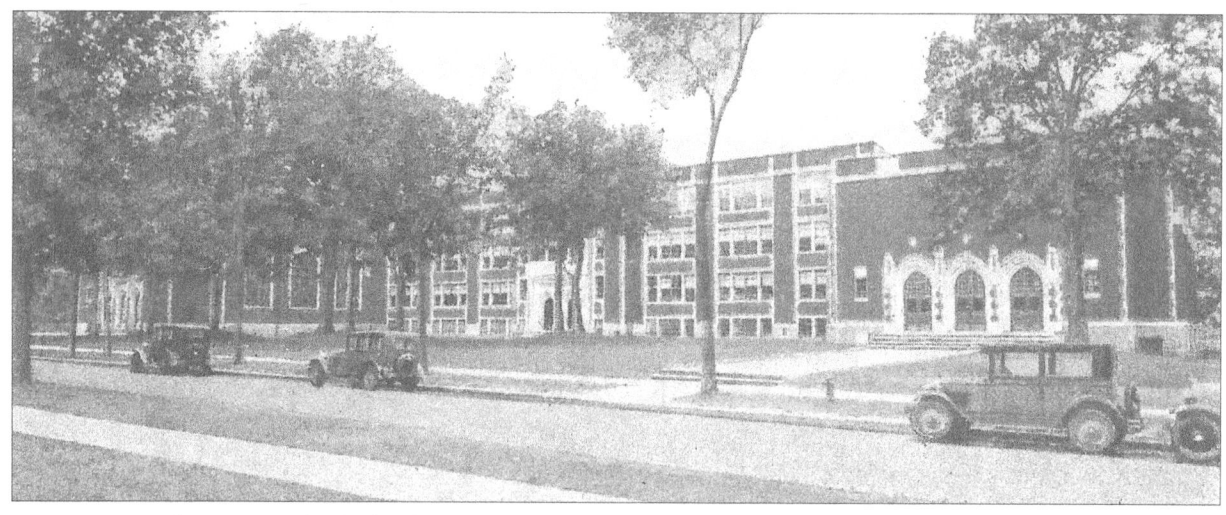

John Deere Jr. High School, Moline, Illinois, as it looked at the time Chuck and Jack Luchsinger were students.

He married Emma Caroline Sadnick in 1940, then served in the army for four years during World War II.

Chuck Luchsinger was honored in 1947 in Lawrence Lariar's *Best Cartoons of the Year* book, and his subsequent 1950 book, *Careers in Cartooning*. Luchsinger did freelance cartoons for a variety of periodicals including *Yank,* and *The Saturday Evening Post*.

Chuck and Emma brought four children into the world: Robert in 1954, William in 1956, Victoria in 1958 and James in 1960.

Chuck Luchsinger's creative talents included the invention of toys. *Life* magazine published a two-page spread on June 25, 1956, featuring Luchsinger and his popular Fiddlestraws toy.

In 1964, Milton Bradley released Luchisinger's Kookie Chicks game, which featured magnetic wands and plastic eggs that could be manipulated. Chuck's talent was also recognized with an appearance on *The Today Show* with host Hugh Downs.

Luchsinger's last toy creation of merit was in 1980, with the release of a Waldo the Dodo bird doll, a character based on *Cartoon Tele-Tales'* postliminary show, *Jolly Gene and His Fun Machine*.

Jack D. Luchsinger, born February 27, 1920, took an interest in theater at an early age. It was while attending Chicago's Goodman Theatre School that he met Helen King, and the two married January 23, 1942. They graduated from the school that same year.

Jack served four years in the military service during World War II. After the war, he and Helen moved to Philadelphia and continued their work in the theatre, which included touring with a summer theatre circuit throughout the Midwest.

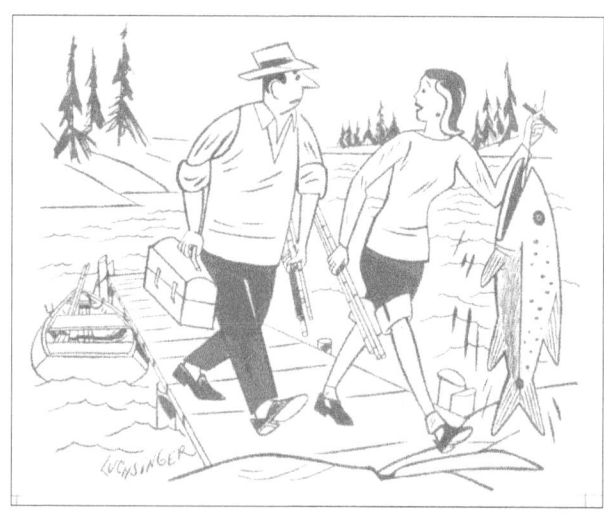

Magazine cartoon illustration by Chuck Luchsinger, circa 1947.

Moving to Long Island, Jack served a stint as stage manager for two Alfred de Liagre Broadway productions in New York.

Luchsinger also conducted some production work for television, including shows like *Stop the Music*, hosted by Bert Parks, and acted in TV shows such as *Robert Montgomery Presents*.

Jack and Helen Luchsinger brought five children into the world: John (affectionately known as Jaxon) in 1944, Jory in 1945, Jay in 1948, Jan in 1950, and Jeffrey in 1958.

After his television productions with brother Chuck, Jack entered the advertising profession as a copywriter and account executive. He and his wife continued their acting interests, performing with little theater groups wherever they lived.

Chuck Luchsinger died March 6, 2009, at the age of 95. Jack Luchsinger died January 29, 2010, at the age of 89. Their sister, Velma (Luchsinger) Stanley, died January 25, 2012, at the age of 96. Their brother, Richard, recently celebrated his 100th birthday, in November, 2017.

Traveling back in time 70 years to the infancy of television broadcasting, the two brothers in early 1948 developed an idea for a children's show. The program, as they imagined it, would combine unique characters, rhyming storytelling, and live illustrations.

Pioneering siblings Chuck and Jack Luchsinger decided to name the show *Cartoon TeleTales*.

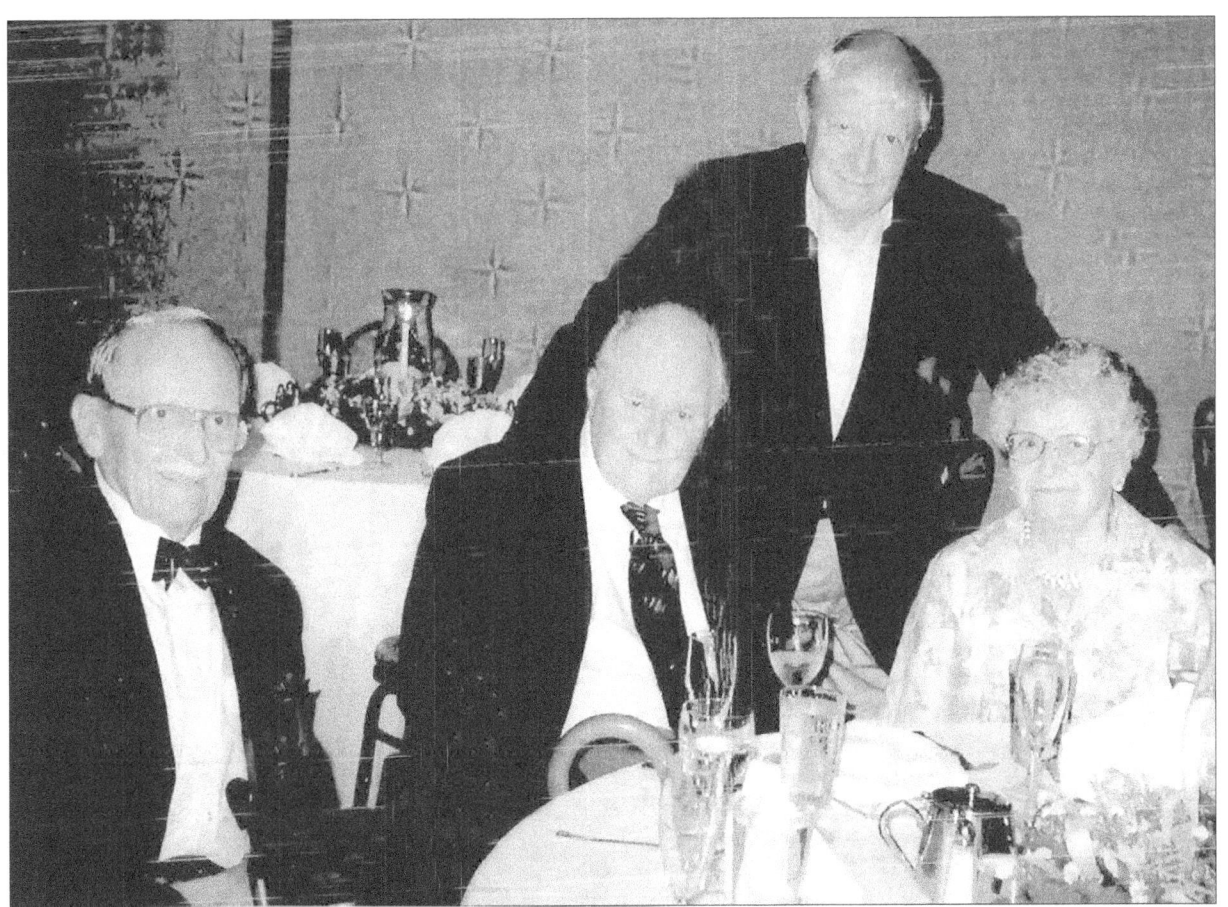

Left to right, Jack and Chuck Luchsinger, with brother Richard (standing) and sister Velma (Luchsinger) Stanley, 2003.

AMERICAN BROADCASTING COMPANY

TELEVISION PRESENTATION

"CARTOON TELETALES"

ORIGINATES: WFIL-TV WEDNESDAY, JUNE 2, 1948
 6:45 - 7:15 P.M., D.S.T.

CAST

CHUCK LUCHSINGER - CARTOONIST
JACK LUCHSINTER - NARRATOR
_____ - CHILD GUEST

WRITTEN BY: CHUCK LUCHSINGER   A.B.C. - TV STAFF:
MUSICAL EFFECTS BY: _____   BABETTE L. HENRY, Director
                                  JEAN HEATON, ASSISTANT

The first two *Cartoon TeleTales* scripts, written by Chuck Luchsinger, that were used when the show moved to Times Square, New York, at the new ABC headquarters. The manuscripts still bear WFIL-TV as the location of production.

CHAPTER TWO
The Genesis of Cartoon TeleTales

It is often said in a world of opportunity that timing is everything. This was true regarding Jack and Chuck Luchsinger during the infancy of original television programming.

In early 1948, Chuck Luchsinger approached his brother Jack with a novel idea for a new television program for children. Chuck, a writer and cartoonist, imagined if he could invent entertaining stories, his brother, Jack, a theatrical actor, could read them while he stood at an easel illustrating the tale in real time.

Each show would introduce original characters, virtually all animals and creatures, in fables with morals. While the show wouldn't present animated cartoons, the brothers were animated enough. Jack delivered tales with the experience as a performer, and Chuck drew a dozen or more illustrations at the speed of lightning.

The program, *Cartoon TeleTales*, would be a living storybook, and an education in illustration, with Chuck providing drawing lessons for young viewers.

Believing the combination was just the type of programming parents desired for their children, the Luchsingers took a huge step. They approached the William Morris Agency for representation. The agency pitched the show to television networks.

"They wanted to go network, instead of local," Bob Luchsinger, son of Chuck, explained. "Local in [Manhattan], New York, was WPIX. They had the option to go with WPIX, or go with the network. They took the network, which was bigger. So, they had to go to Philadelphia, where the ABC network was at the time."

Earlier that year, WFIL, of Philadelphia, Pennsylvania, had completed construction of a new television studio at 46th and Market Streets, momentarily becoming ABC headquarters. Since their launch into television broadcasting the previous year, WFIL primarily aired newsreels and was seeking original programming when the William Morris Agency, on behalf of the Luchsingers, came knocking.

The Luchsingers made a presentation of their show idea to general manager Roger W. Clipp, and Jack Steck, program director. WFIL liked the concept, and carved out a little corner in their studio for the brothers, constructing a simple set and making use of

ABC advertisement in *Variety* announcing *Cartoon TeleTales*.

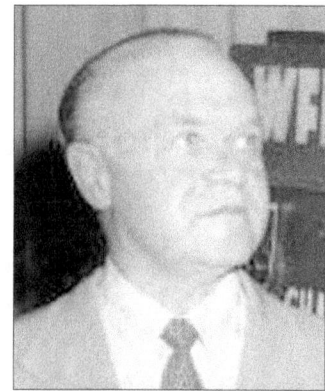
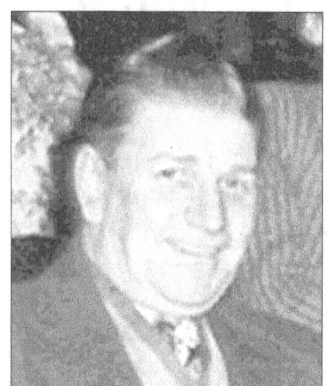
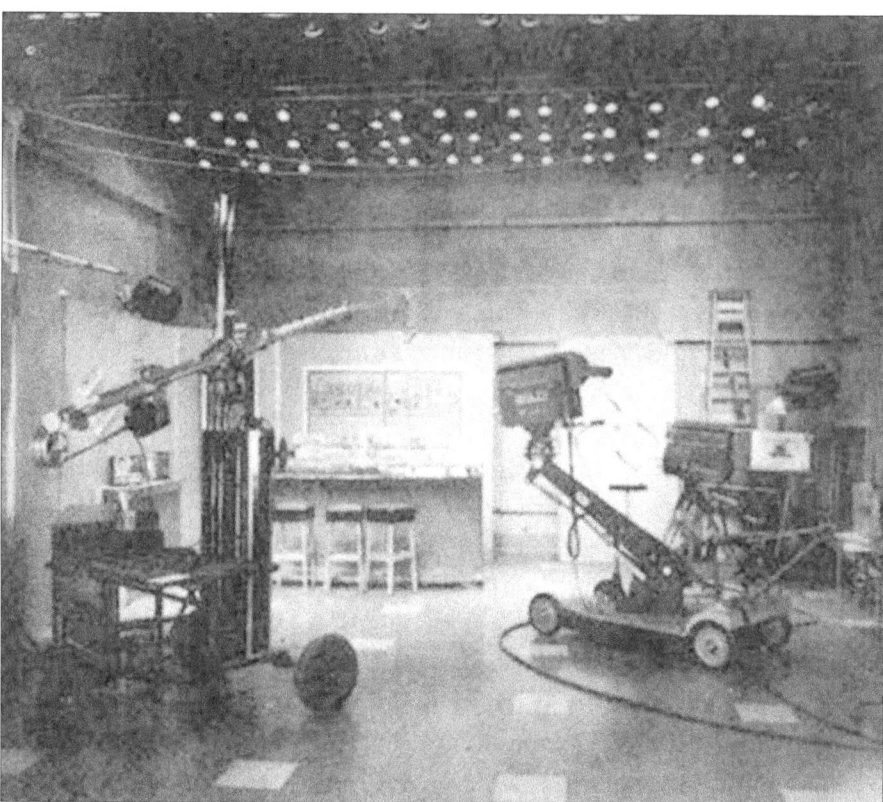

WFIL TV's Roger W. Clipp, left top, and Jack Steck, bottom left. Right, WFIL-TV television studio.in Philadelphia, Pennsylvania, 1948.

one camera.

Chuck Luchsinger got to work inventing amusing characters and turning out scripts, with input from his brother. To add a whimsical delivery, stories were written in rhyme. The poetic aspect added appeal to the tales and became a standard throughout the lifetime of the series.

To prepare artistically for the prospective program, Chuck Luchsinger frequented the Philadelphia Zoo, where he practiced illustrating a variety of animals that would be used as models for characters in the series.

Jack Luchsinger worked on developing character voices, chemistry with his sibling, and rehearsed the presentation, timing the flow of illustrations.

Chuck Luchsinger created a character mascot for the debut of the show, a young boy named Hezekiah, who wore a striped shirt. "Hezzie," as he was nicknamed, was essentially an illustrated co-host and conveyor of wisdom in the 15 minute program.

Cartoon TeleTales made its Philadelphia debut on May 29. Upon its launch, WFIL sales director, John E. Surrick, fielded phone calls from potential sponsors expressing interest in the program.

Television was a relatively new medium at the time, but the American Broadcasting Company committed to being a leader in the growing market. That spring, ABC engaged in a pioneering expansion by constructing a new studio, WJZ-TV, in Times Square, New York. *Variety* magazine reported the facility would be ABC's "new master station," producing content for its affiliates.

ABC headquarters in New York invited the

Luchsingers to their new state-of-the-art studio to produce the program there. The brothers moved back to the Empire state, where their second show originated on June 2.

The ABC network saw great potential in the Luchsinger's routine, as children's television programming, what little that had been achieved, was relegated to story time book reading, adults in costume, and cheesy, uninspiring puppets.

ABC, New York, finalized an agreement with the Luchsingers, making producer Barre Shlaes co-owner of the show. The commitment secured the exclusive rights to all programs originating from the ABC studio. Jack and Chuck Luchsinger maintained exclusive rights to the name, *Cartoon TeleTales*, the show concept, and all stories and characters they created.

Before being appointed producer of *Cartoon TeleTales*, Shlaes was the stage manager for a theatrical production of *Rumpelstiltskin*. Although young at the age of 28, Shlaes saw a future in entertainment and subsequently established Barre Shlaes Theatrical Enterprises based in Los Angeles, CA.

Assigned as the program's director, Babette Henry was no stranger to television. He directed ABC TV's *Tele Tales for Children* in 1945, sort of a predecessor of *Cartoon Tele-Tales*, without live illustration. The show had featured actress and singer, Irene Wicker, and others.

Henry would also direct several other ABC programs during his oversight of *Cartoon TeleTales*, including the short-lived *Photo-Crime*, sponsored and originated by *Look* magazine, based on actual stories. Subsequently, he directed the *Buck Rogers* TV show, which made its debut in 1950, starring Kern Dibbs, and later, Robert Pastene, in the title role.

Jean Heaton became the assistant program director. Heaton had worked on shows such as ABC's *On Trial*, and was director of *The Fitzgeralds*, a favorite talk show that made the transition from radio to TV. It starred Ed and Pegeen Fitzgerald.

ABC arranged for musical accompaniment for the brothers on the set, with the addition

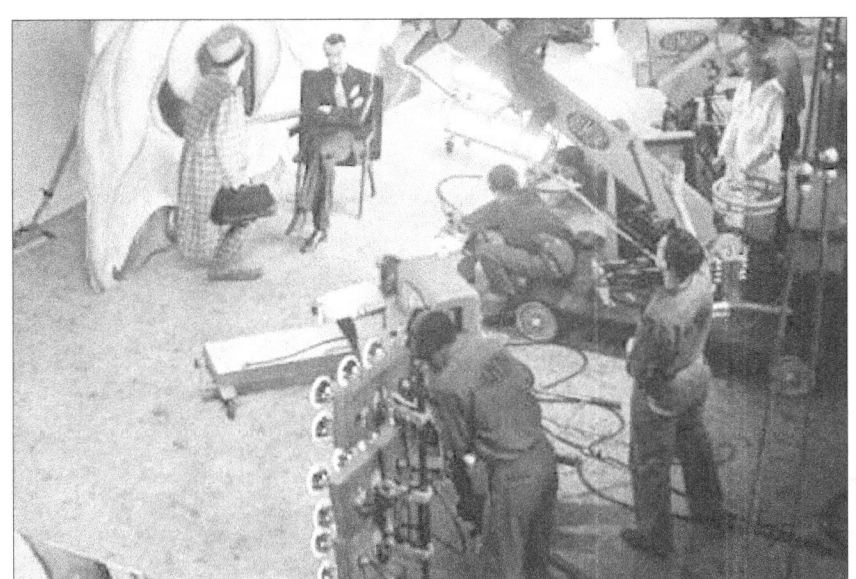
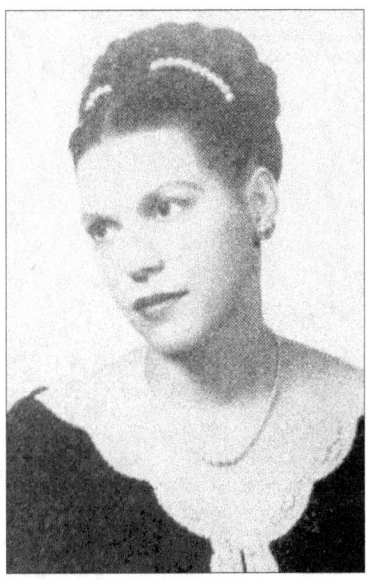

Left, Babette Henry, between camera rigs with arm raised, directs a children's program, 1945. Right, organist Rosa Rio.

On the Air!

WJZ-TV

CHANNEL 7

KEY STATION IN NEW YORK

ABC *TELEVISION NETWORK*

Tuesday, August 10 — a red-letter day in ABC television. Why? Because ABC's key station, WJZ-TV goes on the air in New York... on Channel 7, right smack in the middle of the dial.

For years ABC has been working, planning for network television. (During the early days of telecasting ABC produced more commercial programs, in more cities, for more sponsors, than any other group working in this new medium.) As time went along, ABC assembled a staff of top video experts, and now, at long last, is completely geared for full-schedule, nation-wide television.

On the following pages, you will find the full story of how an exciting, new television network has come into being...

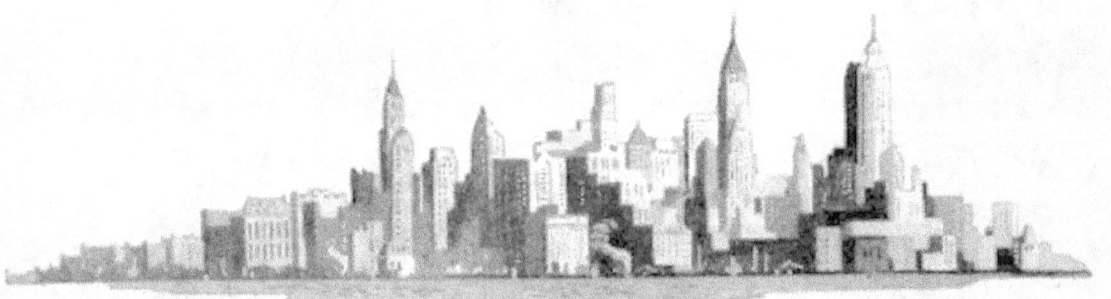

Advertisement announcing the opening of the new WJZ-TV facility, headquarters of the American Broadcasting network, located in Times Square, New York.

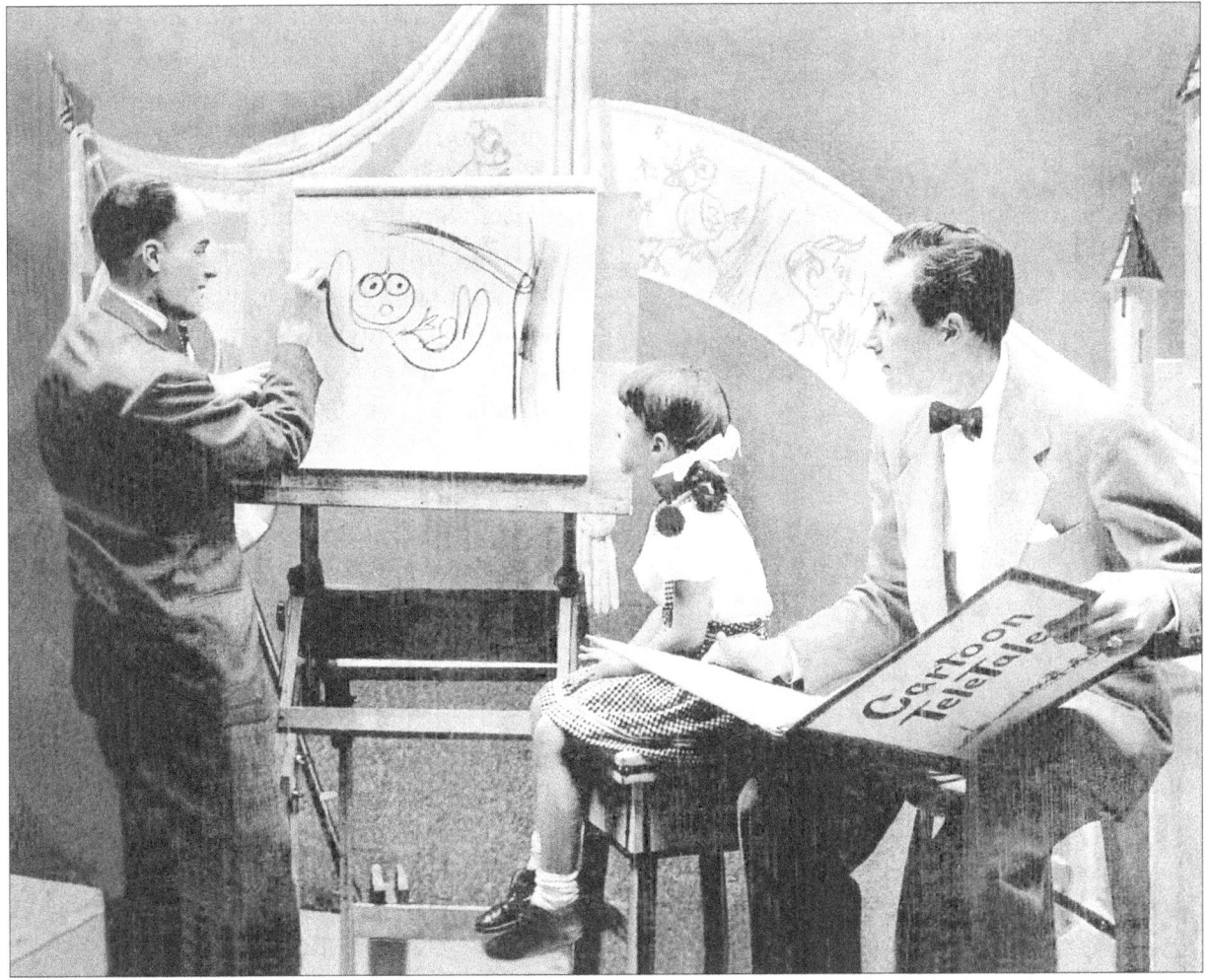

Promotional photo taken on the set of *Cartoon TeleTales*, 1948. Chuck draws, as Jack tells a tale, for a young guest. Photo courtesy of the Luchsinger family.

of motion picture organist Rosa Rio.

Rio, who began her career as a silent film accompanist, composer and arranger, provided a bouncy and whimsical musical backdrop for *Cartoon TeleTales*. At age 46, Rio had spun out musical soundtracks for Buster Keaton, Charles Chaplin, and Al Jolson. Since the demise of silent motion pictures, Rio found steady employment in radio programming.

While the new Central Park facility was structurally complete to facilitate program production, their national broadcasting capability wouldn't be completed for several months. Thus, *Cartoon TeleTales*, which made its Empire State debut on June 2, was initially a local broadcast and remained so for ten weeks.

The premiere show on WJZ-TV featured the tale of Rufus the Rabbit, and reintroduced the series mascot, Hezekiah, who became a series regular, appearing in every subsequent *Cartoon TeleTales* broadcast. The set featured a large backdrop painting of a castle with tall conical pillars, giving the show a fairytale feel.

The show aired once a week late afternoon, and quickly became a regional favorite dur-

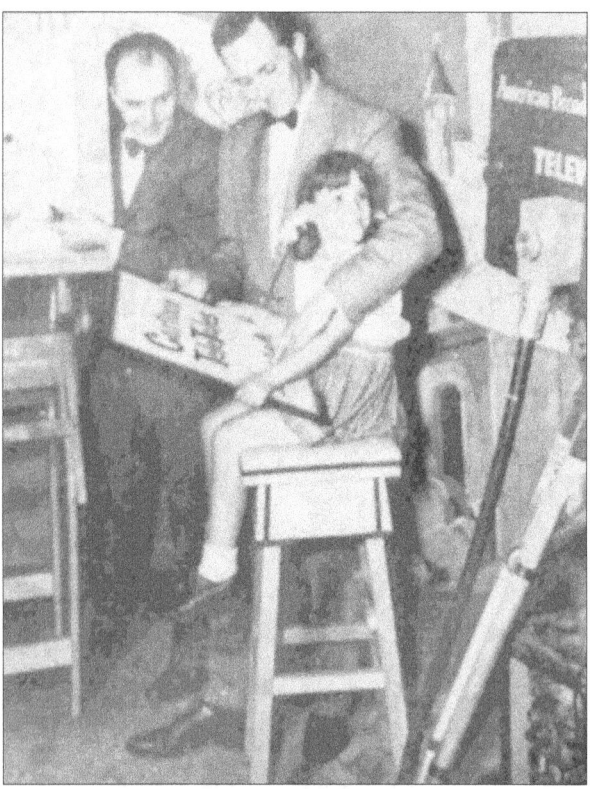

Chuck Luchsinger at the easel, while Jack Luchsinger welcomes a young fan to the show. Photograph reproduced from a magazine.

ing its initial 13-week run. Parents and children were introduced to stories featuring Luchsinger original characters, such as: Fig the Frog, Kornelius the Kangaroo, Little What Am I, Sizzmo the Sky Rocket, Bungle the Beaver, Sippsy the Mosquito, Maurice the Mouse, Yakety-Yak the Pelican, Boo-Golly the Ghost, Wiley the Fox, Hezekiah the Sea-Going Horse, and an adventure starring The Runaway Roller Skates.

Preparations and awareness that the program would go out nationally to ABC affiliates gave the Luchsingers, and the production crew, time to refine the routine, and added an audience participation element. Kids were asked to mail in their drawings of characters the Luchsingers presented, to be put on display in "Chuck and Jack's Art Gallery" segment appearing in every show.

The idea spawned an outpouring of mail to the ABC Times Square studio. Everyone was beginning to see they had a potential hit on their hands. The enthusiasm also made it easy to sell commercial spots, generating sponsors for the program.

Variety magazine reported on July 7, 1948, that commercial advertising time slots for *Cartoon TeleTales* were $500 per show, with a 26-week contract. The sum is the equivalent of over $5,000 today.

ABC's new Times Square television headquarters officially opened on August 10.

Having acquired enough sponsors to make the show viable, WJZ-TV added *Cartoon TeleTales* to their network schedule, and announced the program's availability to affiliates the following day.

Thus, *Cartoon TeleTales* first hit the airwaves on August 11, in the 7:00-7:15 p.m. timeslot as a network program. The show would appear twice weekly, on Monday and Wednesday.

In the first "national broadcast" of *Cartoon TeleTales*, Jack and Chuck Luchsinger presented character Hey You the Lion, featuring the king of the jungle, in a story concerning honesty.

Over the next six weeks, the show introduced characters such as Freebly the Flying Fish, Percy the Pigeon, Leon the Lightning Bug, Usta the Rooster, and Mimi the Mole.

Only weeks into its run, due to enthusiastic viewer response, the program expanded to 30 minutes, every Monday and Wednesday afternoon, at 5:30 p.m.

The expansion was a result of not having enough time in a 15-minute program to adequately accomplish everything. The change allowed more time to exhibit viewer artwork and run contests with prizes. The top prize presented was a drawing package that included just about everything a young, aspiring artist would need.

Variety published a positive review of the Luchsinger brothers, and their show, *Cartoon TeleTales*, on September 1.

"ABC television has taken two surefire gimmicks for kids' shows—fairy tales and cartoon drawings—tossed them in a contest for the moppets and a giveaway and come up with a passably pleasing program in *Cartoon TeleTales*, that should lure its share of the knee-pants and pigtails crowd," *Variety* wrote. "As with most other TV shows slanted at the youngsters, though, it's got nothing to offer any adult viewers."

Variety described the format of the show as fundamentally simple, "as it should be." It also noted, unaware of Jack Luchsinger's theatrical background, the storyteller's performing antics.

"The brother team of Chuck and Jack Lucksinger do all the work, with the former drawing line sketches to illustrate his brother's off-hand yarn spinning," *Variety* conveyed. "Chuck's drawings were much more professional, since the other brother, working sans script, had a habit of fluffing right into the face of the camera. Any suspense in telling was pointed up by the musical blurbs of organist Rosa Rio."

Variety pointed out that favorable response to the show was undeniable, as children had sent in their art for display on the show.

"The fairytale was proceeded with a demonstration of drawings sent in by moppet viewers to be judged for prizes," *Variety* wrote. "The number of drawings on view, incidentally, demonstrated the show has already attracted a number of lookers, despite the fact that WJZ-TV has been on the air only a few weeks."

While *Variety* praised the show for its art instruction aspect, the reviewer mused that perhaps an unskilled novice might be confused by it all.

"Modern art students would probably find some merit in the artwork," *Variety* added, "but it represented just a maze to the uninitiated."

The art gallery, the closing element of the program, quickly defused the notion. The display of illustrations mailed in by young viewers followed instructions, and in many cases, showed creativity and talent.

Until *Cartoon TeleTales*, children's programming was a fragile target for parents and media critics. The shows that had been produced were boring, uninspiring, and had little in the way of creativity to earn a loyal following among moppets. However, within several months, a winning formula had been achieved with the Luchsinger's show.

The brothers were well aware they had a remarkable hit on their hands.

ABC promoted the new show in press releases, calling it "a unique program that keeps kiddies spellbound!"

And spellbound wasn't an exaggerated observation, as letters from young readers began streaming into the ABC studio.

A full-scale reach to all of ABC's network affiliates enabling them to carry *Cartoon TeleTales* wasn't completed until November 20. WFIL-TV in Philadelphia, where the program originated, began broadcasting the Luchsinger's show on that date.

By the end of the year, *Cartoon TeleTales* was receiving over 1,000 pieces of mail per week, virtually all from children, containing drawings.

Cartoonists j.g.

Chuck looked at Jack; Jack looked at Chuck.
"We're naturals for television," said Jack.
"Check," said Chuck.

That was a year ago, and the Luchsinger brothers have been combining their talents ever since for Cartoon Teletales, an ABC network show.

Chuck is a well known cartoonist and Jack is an actor. Chuck draws pictures to illustrate stories that he writes for the show, while Jack reads the stories out of a big book whose very size must delight every child. These Teletales revolve about such interesting characters as Hey You the Lion, Bumsniff the Bloodhound, Hambone the Possum, Herman the Stupid Cupid, and all their kin and neighbors.

The story finished, there's a simple lesson in how to draw the main character. Chuck sets the pace and his young viewers draw right along with him. They send these efforts in, and those judged good enough for the "art gallery" are rewarded with a drawing pencil. The "artist of the week" rates a special drawing kit.

And don't think only the kiddies send in their stuff. For instance, 7-year-old Gail Rafferty sent a fine drawing of Torpy the Turtle. Along with it came a similar effort signed "John Rafferty, Gail's Dad." Chuck thinks Gail's drawing has a slight edge.

Producer of Cartoon Teletales is Barre Schlaes, and the time is Sunday evening, 6 P.M. EDT, 5 P.M. CDT, over the ABC eastern and midwest networks.

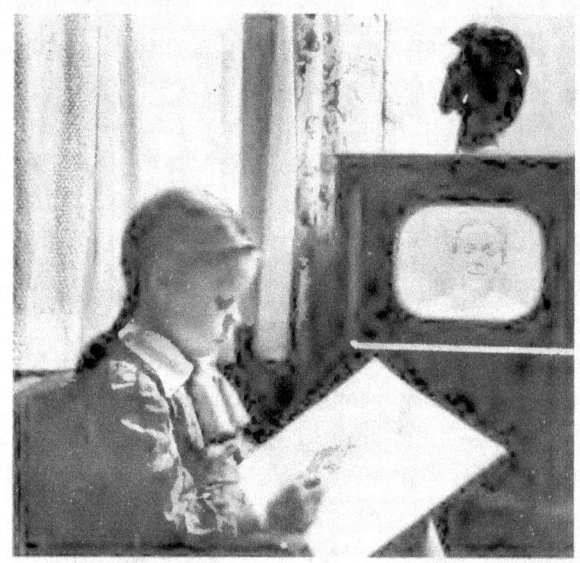

Six-year-old "art student" Ruth Lawrence works hard over the cartoon that may win her the title "artist of the week."

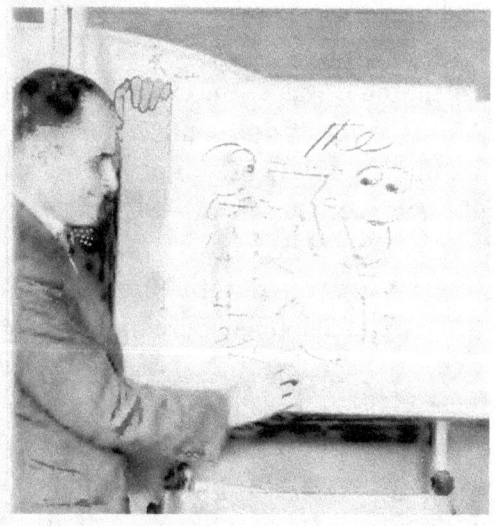

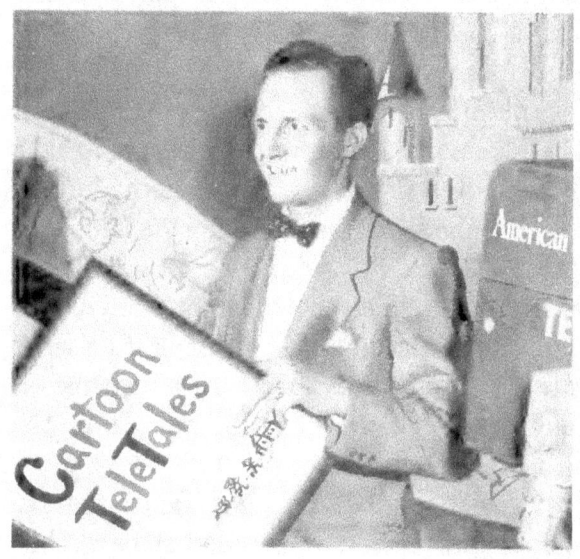

Jack and Chuck Luchsinger find ABC's Cartoon Teletales a perfect medium for their talents. Chuck (left), draws the cartoons; Jack (above), reads the story against the castle backdrop which enchants young listeners.

RADIO MIRROR TELEVISION SECTION

Feature page in Radio and Television Mirror, June 1949.

CHAPTER THREE

TeleTales Gains Critical Acclaim

The Luchsinger brothers welcomed in 1949 with a special New Year's edition of *Cartoon TeleTales* broadcast on December 26. The show featured a special guest, one-year-old Jay Luchsinger.

Jay, the son of Jack Luchsinger, was indeed a New Year's baby, born January 1, 1948.

Dressed only in a diaper and wearing a hat adorned with a 1949 banner, the tot has no memory of his network television debut. But nearly 70 years since the event, he's heard enough tales about it.

"My dad managed to talk my mom into letting him use me as a prop on the show," Jay Luchsinger said. "Uncle Chuck drew an illustration for the story/script they had written for the occasion."

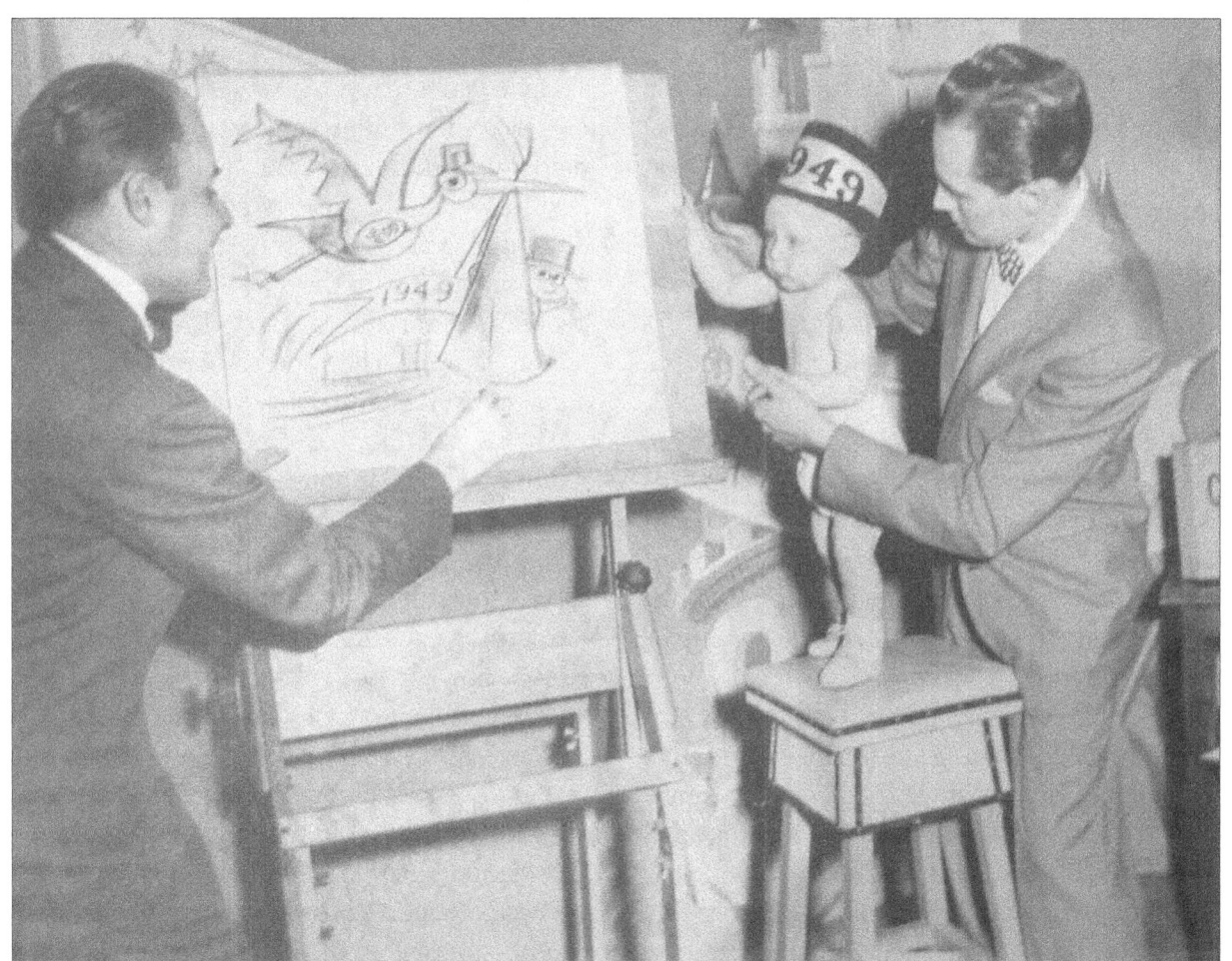

Chuck Luchsinger, left, illustrates, while baby Jay, held by his father Jack Luchsinger, right, watches during the December 26, 1948 broadcast of *Cartoon TeleTales*. Photo courtesy of the Luchsinger family.

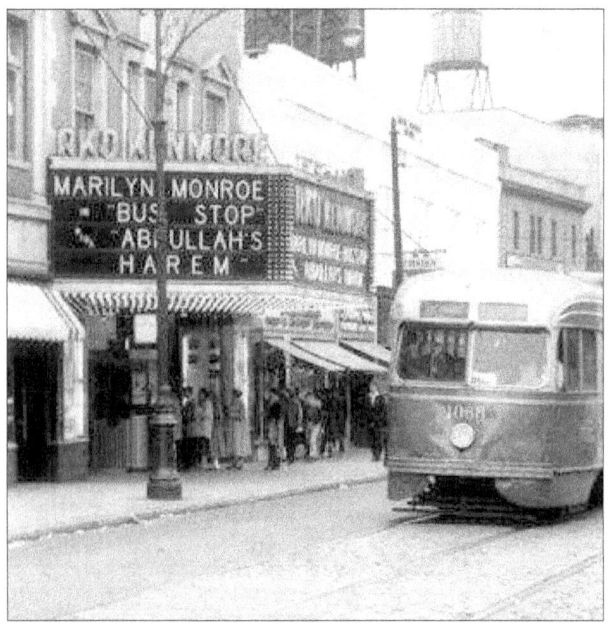 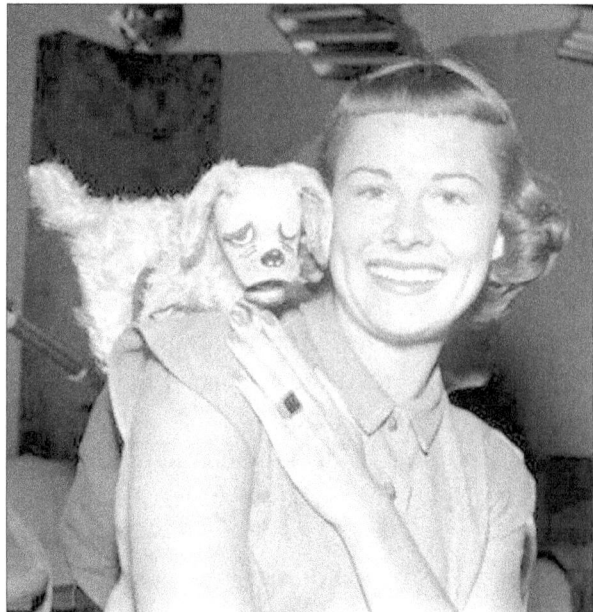

The RKO Kenmore Theater, left, in the 1950's. Doris Brown, left, hostess of the show Lucky Pup, with the star puppet on her shoulder.

Standing on a stool, safely supported by his father's arms, Jay watched "Uncle Chuck" draw a character named B-36 the Stork, while his dad told the tale of the baby-delivering bird. Chuck Luchsinger had named the stork after the World War II bomber, the Convair B-36 Peacemaker.

One significant thing to celebrate at the dawn of the new year was *Cartoon TeleTales'* move to a critical primetime family viewing spot, Sunday evenings from 6:00-6:30. Instead of airing shows during busy school and homework weekdays, the network realized greater audience potential once every Sunday, when families slowed down and gathered together.

This year, the Luchsingers cranked out stories and illustrations featuring characters such as: Herman the Stupid Cupid, Upsie Doozy the Giraffe, Mozart the Mocking Bird and Little Slivers the Porcupine.

Billboard magazine published a favorable review of the show in their January 29, 1949 issue, noting the stories were "told and sketched effectively."

"Two other gimmicks permit audience participation," *Billboard* said. "One is an art gallery in which kid viewers send in their own drawings, and the other is a lesson in cartooning, in which the two brothers on the program team up to show the youngsters how to simplify the process of cartooning. It adds up to an okay session."

The *Child Study Association of America*, in its 1949 annual published report issued to parents, gave *Cartoon TeleTales* a glowing recommendation. The organization, which conducted studies and presented evaluations concerning educational values, complimented the show regarding its delivery.

"The amusing stories are accompanied by cartoons swiftly and cleverly sketched as the tale unfolds," the reported stated. "Viewers are then instructed in how to draw these cartoons and invited to send in their drawings."

Variety reported, on February 9, *Cartoon TeleTales'* growing popularity with moppets.

"Many success stories have been told about

television commercial shows, but here's one on a sustainer," *Variety* said. "*Cartoon TeleTales* aired Sunday nights over ABC TV's eight-station tie-up, plus two outlets getting the show via kinescope recordings, this week came up with a mail pull of 3,728 letters."

The storytelling showman aspect regarding *Cartoon TeleTales*, thanks to the acting and stage experience of Jack Luchsinger, would propel the brothers before theater audiences in early 1949.

Variety reported in their March 2 issue that the pair were scheduled to appear live in Brooklyn, taking their act to the stage, at least for a "one-shot" engagement.

"On television, in addition to reviving old Vaudeville acts for theater dates is furthering the resurgence of live theatrical shows with talent developed on its own," *Variety* explained. "For example, Chuck and Jack Luchsinger, who are co-emcees on ABC TV's *Cartoon TeleTales*, are scheduled for an experimental one-shot appearance on stage of the RKO Kenmore, Brooklyn, March 12."

The RKO Kenmore, which opened in 1928, was initially a vaudeville and movie house for the B.F. Keith Circuit. Located at 2101 Church Street, the RKO Kenmore, which seated 2,400 patrons, had seen better days, but still was a favorite theater. The establishment was mainly engaged in the projection of motion pictures, but hosted regional plays.

"The theater has ballyhooed the show with handbills and newspaper ads, and if it proves successful, the team will be booked on the entire RKO metropolitan circuit," *Variety* stated.

The Luchsinger's booking at the RKO Kenmore also was in response to competing television network CBS, which had taken one of its shows onto the stage.

"The same house recently booked recently CBS TV's *Lucky Pup* show for its stage, bringing back the program several weeks later for a repeat," *Variety* stated. "Luchsingers will duplicate their Sunday evening video program, drawing sketches to the accompaniment of story-telling for the moppet audience."

Hope and Morey Bunin's children's show, about a dog that inherited $5 million from a circus queen, involved hand-manipulated puppets as the program stars. Part of the puppet's appeal was that their faces had mobile devices to create facial expressions.

Following the popularity of *Kukla, Fran, and Ollie*, puppet shows were standard children's fare in TV programming. However, *Lucky Pup* was one of the more popular shows, and competing for advertising dollars made kid's show producers competitive.

The kid's market was expanding and appealing to advertisers, as long as ratings and popularity were high. Over the following two years, ABC, CBS, and NBC combined broadcast 27 hours of children's programming per week. The trend took a nosedive after 1951, when advertisers shifted their sponsorship to adult programming.

The positive response and reception of the Luchsingers at the RKO Kenmore Theater had ABC executives dreaming up other ways to promote the talented brothers. In particular, Chuck, the artist.

ABC utilized Chuck Luchsinger as a guest, appearing on several other programs they produced for broadcast. On May 14, 1949, Luchsinger performed on the second episode of *Stop the Music*, hosted by Bert Parks, presenting a drawing demonstration. The program was a predecessor of *Name that Tune*.

The Luchsinger brothers knew Parks, and

Jack had worked on production for the show.

Variety saw the appearance of the cartoonist on *Stop the Music* as a way for ABC to repurpose those on their payroll.

"Last Thursday's session [of *Stop the Music*] showed a slight attempt to economize in using Chuck Luchsinger for more visualization," *Variety* said. "But others had their full share of the show, too."

The press and entertainment periodicals took more of an interest in *Cartoon TeleTales* and the Luchsingers as the program approached its first year anniversary.

Variety reported on May 4, in celebration of the first anniversary, the program was promoting a "special election." Hosts Jack and Chuck Luchsinger were asking viewers to cast ballots over the next three weeks to pick their favorite story out of the 60 tales spun by Jack Luchsinger.

Billboard recognized the first anniversary of *Cartoon TeleTales* in their June 4 edition, stating the show had "marked its first birthday on May 29," harkening back to the time when the show originated from Philadelphia.

Radio and Television Mirror presented a feature in their June 1949, issue observing the show's anniversary.

"Chuck looked at Jack; Jack looked at Chuck. 'We're naturals for television,' said Jack. 'Check,' said Chuck," is how the article began.

"That was a year ago, and the Luchsinger brothers have been combining their talents ever since, for *Cartoon TeleTales*, an ABC network show," *Radio and Television Mirror* reported. "Chuck is a well-known cartoonist, and Jack is an actor. Chuck draws pictures to illustrate stories that he writes for the show, while Jack reads the stories out of a big book whose very size must delight every child."

Radio and Television Mirror named several of the "interesting characters" appearing in tales, such as Hey You the Lion, Bumsniff the Bloodhound, Hambone the Possum, and Herman the Stupid Cupid.

"When the story finished, there's a simple lesson in how to draw the main character. Chuck sets the pace, and his young viewers draw right along with him," *Radio and Television Mirror* explained. "They send these efforts in, and those judged good enough for the 'art gallery' are rewarded with a drawing pencil."

Radio and Television Mirror reported the lucky candidate chosen "artist of the week" received a special drawing kit. The magazine also pointed out that it wasn't just children who were interacting with *Cartoon TeleTales*.

"Don't think only the kiddies send in their stuff," the magazine said. "For instance, 7-year-old Gail Rafferty sent a fine drawing of Torpy the Turtle and along with it came a similar effort signed 'John Rafferty, Gail's Dad.'"

Chuck Luchsinger jokingly stated to the reporter that he "thinks Gail's drawing has a slight edge" in the contest.

With the overwhelming response from young viewers, a notion was entertained to invite a small number of children, ages 4 to 7, onto the set during the live telecast. Within short order, Jack Luchsinger announced to young viewers that they could write in for free tickets to appear in the moppet audience on the show. Of course, asking one's parent was imperative.

Children on the set were there to listen to storyteller Jack Luchsinger and watch as Chuck illustrated the tale. Then came a more hands-on aspect, when Chuck presented an art lesson, showing kids how to draw the program's featured character.

Variety reviewed *Cartoon TeleTales* a second time in their July 27, 1949 issue. This time, they acknowledged the success of the program, stating it "had caught on with viewers," and in recognition, ABC had renewed the show for another season.

"*Cartoon TeleTales*, a half-hour show airing Sunday evenings via ABC TV, is going into its second straight year as one of the better shows for moppets," *Variety* stated. "In addition to being entertaining, this one has the added advantage of including a drawing lesson for the pint-sized viewers, capably explained and demonstrated by cartoonist Chuck Luchsinger. His brother, Jack, has a neat flair for reading fairy tales to the kids, which are illustrated in a sort of running commentary by the cartoonist at his drawing board."

Children being on the set had added a personal element, displaying not only wonder but inspiration, and *Variety* didn't overlook the fact.

"On last Sunday's program, the cameras were put to good advantage in picking up the rapt faces of four moppets brought in as studio guests as they listened to the story," *Variety* stated. "The brothers then displayed their 'art gallery,' featuring some of the best pictures sent in by home viewers, each of whom gets a drawing kit as a prize."

Variety then gave the program a ringing endorsement for sponsors.

"The program, which is good enough to rate sponsorship, is packaged by indie producer Barre Shlaes."

The observation of *Cartoon TeleTales'* anniversary didn't go unnoticed by *Sponsor* magazine, either, which reported the astounding numbers regarding viewer interaction.

"In the last year 75,000 youngsters drew and submitted cartoon illustrations of figures appearing on ABC's *Cartoon TeleTales*," *Sponsor* reported. "Simple drawing instruction is part of the show."

Perhaps as an act of relaxation and celebration, Chuck Luchsinger took a week off, having artist Ed Nofziger take his place for one show. *Variety* reported on the substitute in its August 10 issue.

"Ed Nofziger, the cartoonist, is subbing for Chuck Luchsinger on ABC's *Cartoon TeleTales* this Sunday (Aug. 14) while the latter takes his first vacation since the show premiered 15 months ago," *Variety* said.

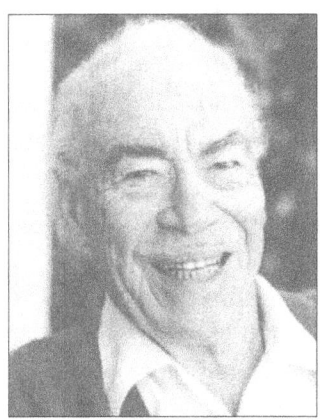

Ed Nofziger, later in life.

Nofziger, who began his career as an illustrator in 1938 for the *Saturday Evening Post*, entered the field of animation after service in World War II. Working at UPA Studios illustrating *Mr. Magoo*, he created the character, Mother Magoo.

Subsequently, Nofziger worked at Hanna-Barbera on *Ruff and Ready*, and later wrote scripts for Walt Disney comic books.

In its September issue, *Radio and Television Mirror* that reported *Cartoon TeleTales* had reached back on its anniversary, pulling out 55 Luchsinger characters created during the program's duration, and conducted a poll with viewers. Which character do you like best? The magazine reported the winning result.

"Boo-Golly the Ghost won out [against] fifty-four other cartoon characters in *Cartoon TeleTales'* polls of its loyal viewers," *Radio and Television Mirror* reported. "Not even with the other delightful *TeleTales* character, Hey You the Lion, or the impressive Bumsniff the Bloodhound, came close to the ectoplasmic Boo-Golly when all the votes were counted."

The contest concluded weeks earlier, but the flood of mail proved to be a time-consuming task, counting and tallying all of the ballots.

The program had generated a lot of revenue and interest, but ABC announced the show would be cancelled the end of summer. *Cartoon TeleTales'* final broadcast was on Sunday, September 25, 1949.

It didn't appear to have been the network's decision, but rather the Luchsinger brothers interest in pursuing other projects. And there were enough snippets in periodicals to support the notion.

When not on the set of *Cartoon TeleTales*, the Luchsingers had individually engaged in other artistic pursuits.

The summer of 1949, Jack Luchsinger returned to the stage, acting in summer theater presentations in Westbury, at Winthrop Hall Playhouse, performing with Edward Watson.

Chuck Luchsinger had been pursuing commercial illustration opportunities, and in the field of television advertising.

Variety reported on September 14, 1949 that Chuck Luchsinger's artistic talent was being put to use in Admiral television advertisements. According to the publication, Luchsinger was "doing quick sketch commercials" for the electrical appliance company.

ABC hadn't slammed the door on the brothers. In fact, they left it open with an extended invitation to return.

Viewer mail kept arriving at ABC headquarters, even though the program was off the air, and positive reports and praise from academics concerning *Cartoon TeleTales* continued through the end of the year.

The National Council of Teachers of English recognized *Cartoon Teletales* in its 1949 annual report, *Elementary English*.

"A top program for youngsters is *Cartoon TeleTales*, which originates in the studios of WJZ-TV in New York. It brings Chuck and Jack Luchsinger to the drawing boards for a brisk half-hour of fun and stories and drawing lessons, with attractive prizes for children who send in the best crayon and pencil illustrations."

In the spring of 1950, the Luchsingers were wooed back by ABC to resurrect *Cartoon TeleTales*. The program would not be part of ABC's regularly scheduled programming, but as "a summer replacement." The show would only air for four months.

After an eight-month absence, *Cartoon TeleTales* returned to the airwaves in late May with all-new shows.

Added to the set of the show midway during its summer run was a large table in the Cartooner's Corner for young artists to sit at while they drew. Previously, kids had used a small board on their laps. The addition not only made it easier for the children to sketch, but the table, strewn with paper and pencils, looked great as a prop.

Children on the set were even encouraged to draw along with the story time segment, before the drawing lesson, with a roving camera capturing more images of the guests exercising their creativity.

Cartoon TeleTales' return was both a welcome and a farewell.

CHAPTER FOUR

Chuck Luchsinger Tells the TeleTale

In early 1950, Dodd, Mead & Company published *Careers in Cartooning*, written by Lawrence Lariar. The author, a cartoonist, became popular for his *Best Cartoons of the Year* series, which published a volume every year from 1942 to 1971. *Careers in Cartooning* featured a chapter about cartooning for television, with Chuck Luchsinger, written by the artist. In it, he explained the genesis and execution of *Cartoon TeleTales*.

In Lariar's introduction for the chapter, he recognized Chuck Luchsinger for his talent and achievements.

"Beginners must not be confused by Chuck Luchsinger's modest account of his successful rise in television," Lariar wrote. "Before he attempted to make the grade in the new medium, he was already a successful cartoonist and commercial artist. His technique in magazine cartooning was almost made-to-order for television, since he always produced cartoons for publication that were both amusing and skillfully drawn. His popularity as a television artist begins here, for the quick cartoons he puts down for the camera are executed with a boldness and simplicity that would look as well in a magazine or a juvenile book as on the video screen."

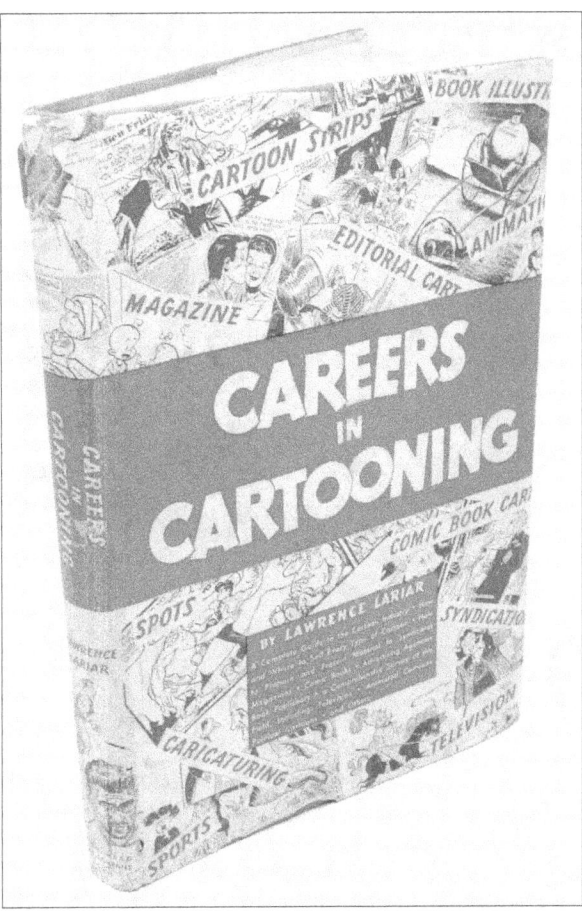

The book by Lawrence Lariar that Chuck Luchsinger appears in.

TELEVISION CARTOONING
From the book Careers in Cartooning
© 1950 Lawrence Lariar
Written by Chuck Luchsinger

Television is undoubtedly the most exciting invention since the invention of the wheel. That's how I felt about it the day I happened to be flipping through a magazine and spied a photo of a cartoonist working before a television camera. I had noticed on numerous occasions, when people had peered over my shoulder into my sketchbook at the zoo or on the street, that the rapid execution of a drawing held the fascination for them akin to magic.

I soon evolved several ideas for television and before long one of my ideas had grown to the stature of a full-fledged outline and well on its way to the stage of discussion.

This involved my brother Jack, who is the actor in the family. Roughly, the basic idea was that he would write animal stories for children and illustrate them before the camera in chalk-talk fashion. Jack would do the narration and act as the master of ceremonies simultaneously with my sketching.

Undaunted by the fact that neither one of us had produced a television show before, we

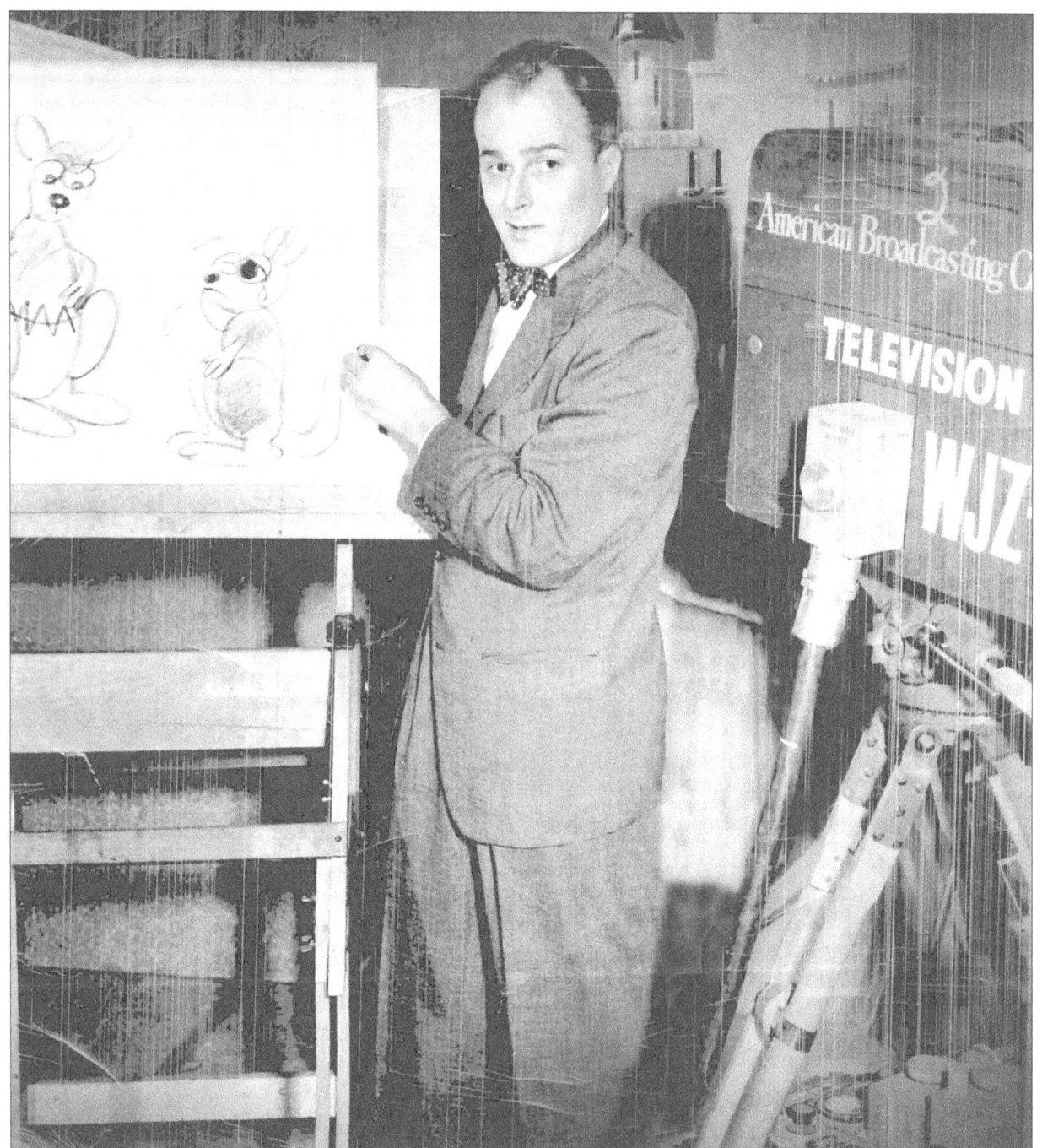

Chuck Luchsinger, on the set of *Cartoon TeleTales*, points to his drawing of Kornelius, the Kangaroo, and friend, June 1948.

made it our business to watch a few of them and then set down our conclusions. Our first decision was that television is an extremely intimate medium which would require, above all else, an intimate approach and the absolute ultimate sincerity.

Secondly, it seemed obvious that things would have to move along quickly on the program, especially visually, since the ear can listen to much and hear nothing, but the eye is a constant critic. With this accumulation of "know-how," we proceeded with our plans.

Naturally a title was our first concern and, in some respects, our first mistake.

The make-up of *TeleTales* is an obvious wedding of television and tales, and the word Cartoon is even more self-explanatory. At the time, it seemed *Cartoon TeleTales* would be an ideal title, but since then we've felt we did not apply the first of our two rules in creating the title for our show.

In other words, *Cartoon TeleTales* is rather cold and too suggestive of animated film strips, rather than the intimate narration and personal illustration of a story. But we had a title—*Cartoon TeleTales*.

Next came the elements to make up the program. We decided on audience-participation, the well-proven gimmick particularly successful in radio. Since our program was to involve an artist, what could possibly be more natural than including a drawing lesson. To give the audience participation gimmick what might possibly be a new twist, we also included an art gallery in which were to be shown drawings sent in by viewers who had participated in the previous week's drawing lesson.

Then, of course, the third element of our proposed half-hour show was to be the story around which both the drawing lesson and art

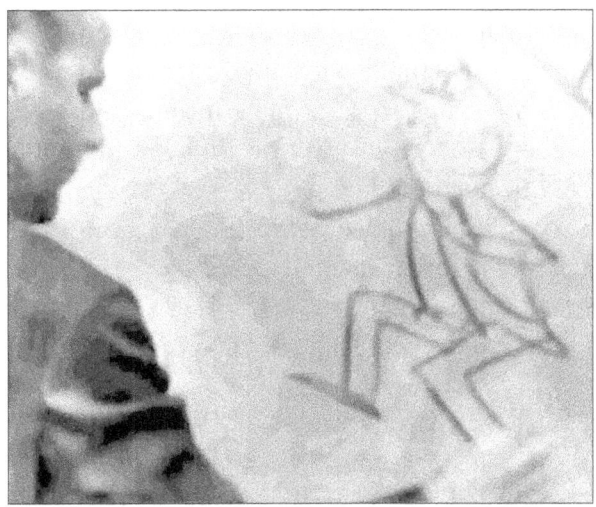

Chuck Luchsinger draws on *Cartoon TeleTales*.

gallery would revolve. With a general zoological background and a natural interest in animals, along with having made countless sketches at the zoos, I decided to write a different story each week, each story to involve a different animal, bird, fish, fowl.

The story would include a few of the habits and characteristics of the creature, and if a moral presented itself, so much the better. First, last and above all, the story was to be funny and to include as many gags as possible in picture and narration.

The story would consist of from ten to fourteen quick-sketch illustrations. Each sketch would last about sixty seconds and the narration accompanying it would be tailored to the time needed for the sketch.

The drawing lesson was also to be kept humorous and the subject was to be the central character in the story for that particular program. He would be doing something funny, and the kids would be encouraged to incorporate ideas of their own into their drawings.

Since the art gallery could hardly be more than a showing of the winning drawings, we encouraged variety in the drawings to help make the art gallery worth-while to watch for those not actually participating in that part of the program. To accentuate intimacy, the art gallery was given the title *Chuck and Jack's Art Gallery.*

In their intended order, a run down of the elements to be included would be:
1. Introduction
2. Chuck and Jack's Art Gallery
3. Story time
4. Drawing lesson
5. Closing

To make up for any lack of sustained interest occasioned by having a new and different story each week, we would include a "hint" in the form of a semi-completed drawing of the character for the following week's story, with much ado about it between Jack and myself and the audience."

We worked out several scripts, rehearsed them thoroughly and approached William Morris Agency with them. As our agent they, in turn, sold *Cartoon TeleTales* to the ABC Network (American Broadcasting Company). And so began the long and happy television life of Chuck and Jack and *Cartoon TeleTales.*

A few of the things we have learned during the many telecasts we have made are as follows:

After much experimenting, it developed that the best type of drawing pad to use was a bond paper of gray or light blue color, glued on the long edge so that the pages can be flipped back over the top of the drawing board rather than ripped from the pad in a disquieting manner during the show.

Speed of execution is the prime requisite when working for the television audience, which, of course, means that the drawings should be kept as simple as possible.

When cartooning for the television camera, always remember to work from right to left, if right-handed, and vice versa, if left-handed, in order to let the audience see the different stages of your work as you finish it. The composition of the picture should be worked out in such a way as to make the right-to-left sequence the easiest and most natural way to draw it.

All in all, the television artist would seem to be a peculiar breed, a combination of quick-sketch artist and actor. He must be able to think on his feet or, even better, on his toes, since the drawings should be executed with a split-second tempo in order to sustain interest.

This leaves little time for thought as to composition and other artistic problems during the finishing of the picture. All such details must be thought out and rehearsed thoroughly before the show goes on.

Writing for television in its physical make-up involves dividing the page into two columns: the column on the right to contain the audio, or narration, and the column on the left to contain the video instructions, such as camera shots, director's cues, music and sound effects, etc.

Other than that, writing for television should meet very much the same requirements as writing for stage or vaudeville, keeping in mind the all-important fact that the eventual audience will see and hear what is being written.

Acting for television presents problems, a subject on which I will not pretend to be an authority; and my only advice to artists who choose to televise their talents is to be doing something, saying something, or drawing something at all times to keep the audience entertained.

CHAPTER FIVE
TeleTales Surviving Episode Pictorial

Cartoon enthusiasts and historians who expect to see a *Cartoon TeleTales* DVD or shows to emerge on YouTube shouldn't hold their breath. While ABC produced Kinescopes of the program, the films apparently are lost to time.

According to the Luchsinger family, two episodes on film survive. One, recorded the summer of 1950, in the private collection of the Luchsinger family, is represented here.

Apparently, Jack Luchsinger gained possession of the shows on film, as a keepsake. One film was transferred to VHS videotape years ago, and subsequently went digital.

The single episode, "Herkimer, the Toad," runs 23 minutes, and does not include the program sponsors. Access was gained by the author to view the episode via a private link provided by the Luchsinger family.

For this book, screen grabs with accompa-

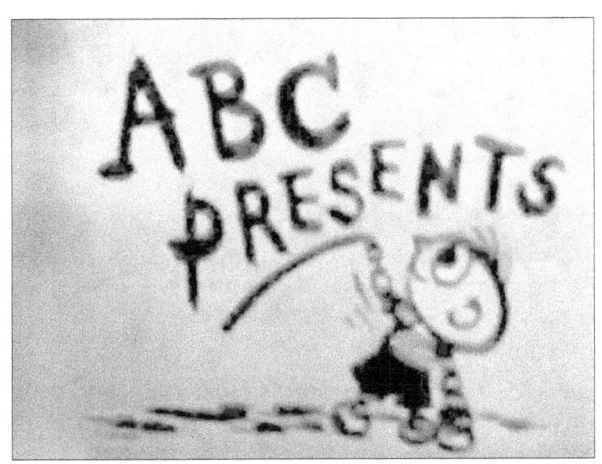
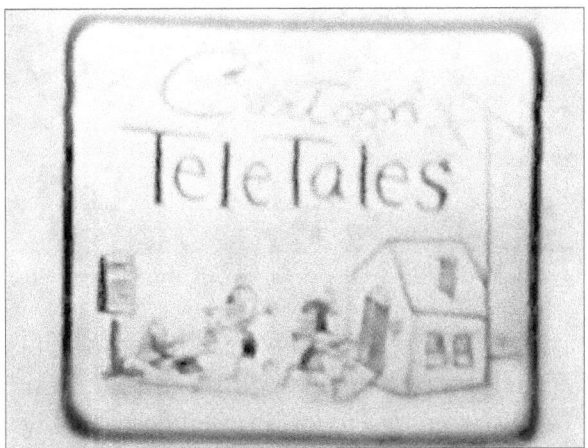
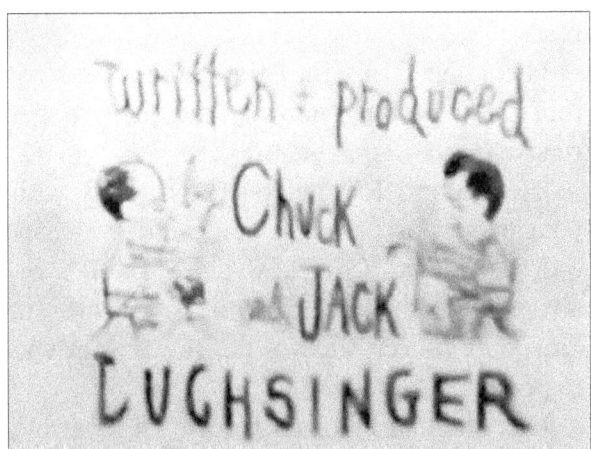
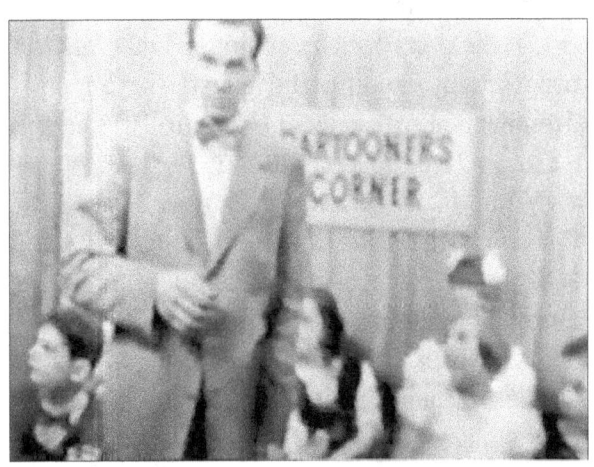

Program's opening credits, and Jack Luchsinger welcomes viewers to the show,

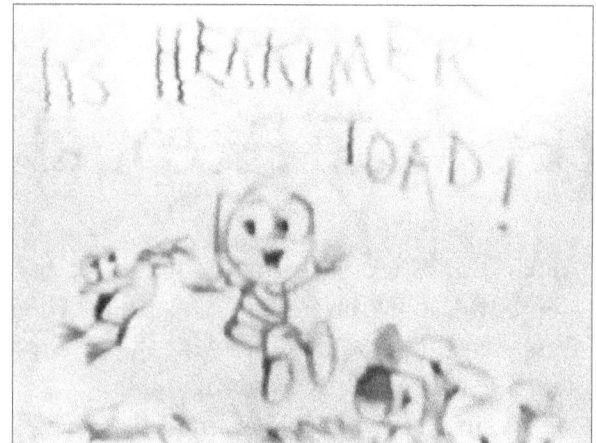 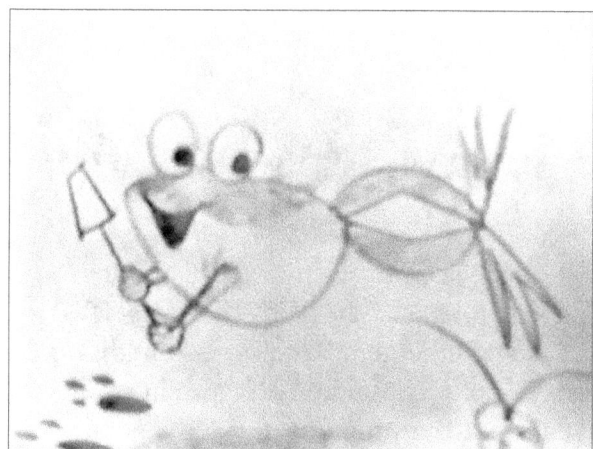
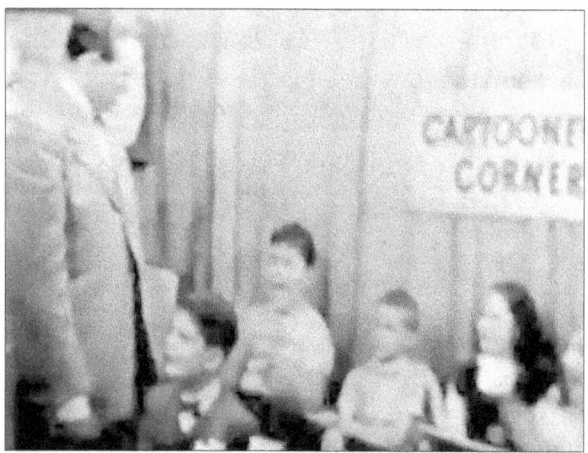 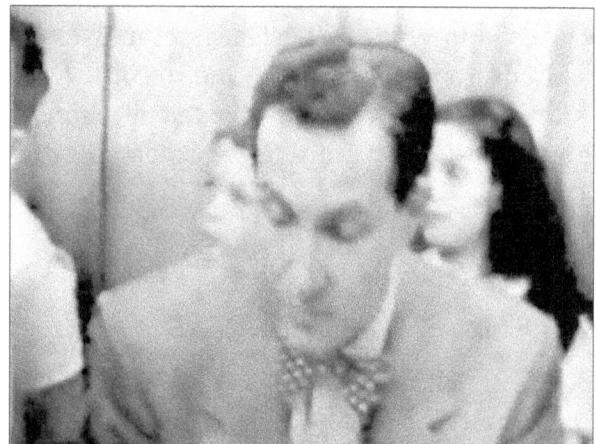

Jack Luchsinger addresses the kids in the Cartooner's Corner to get ready for today's story, the n begins telling the tale of Herkimer the Toad.

nying narrative bring the episode back to life.

The program opens with the title *Cartoon TeleTales* in the form of an illustration by Chuck Luchsinger, depicting the show mascot, Hezekiah. Jack Luchsinger kicks off the program by leading the guests, seven children in the Cartooner's Corner, in singing the *Cartoon TeleTales* theme song.

"What is it?" Jack Luchsinger asks. "It's Car-toon Tele-Tales time," all sing.

Jack announces, "In order to let our friend Hezekiah get his two-cents' worth in here, let's give him a chance to say 'Hello.'"

The camera switches to show Chuck Luchsinger at the easel, standing beside a drawing of Hezekiah and a word balloon of wisdom.

"Hello, Jack, and here's Hezekiah, and he's saying, 'Hi, kids,'" Jack responds. "And he's also saying, 'Have your paper and pencil ready.'"

Jack then looks into the camera and reminds the young viewing audience to get ready.

"Hezzie and I want you to be ready with your paper and pencil so you can draw a cartoon along with Chuck," Jack says. "He's really going to show you how to draw a cartoon, kids, and it's very easy to do, so we want you to be ready for it."

Jack then announces before the drawing lesson, "It's time for this episode's story."

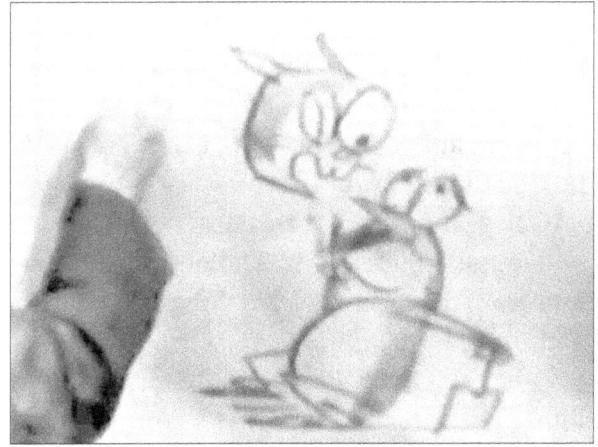 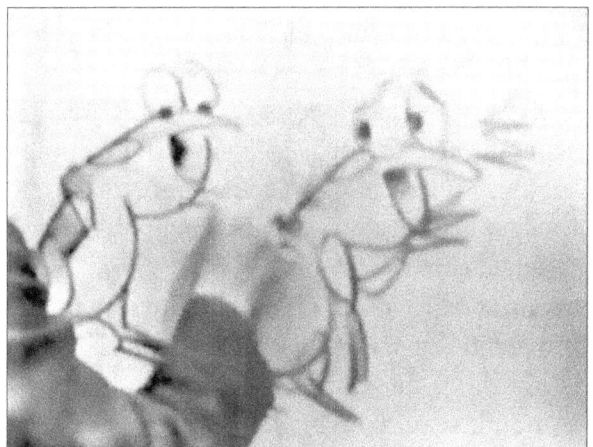
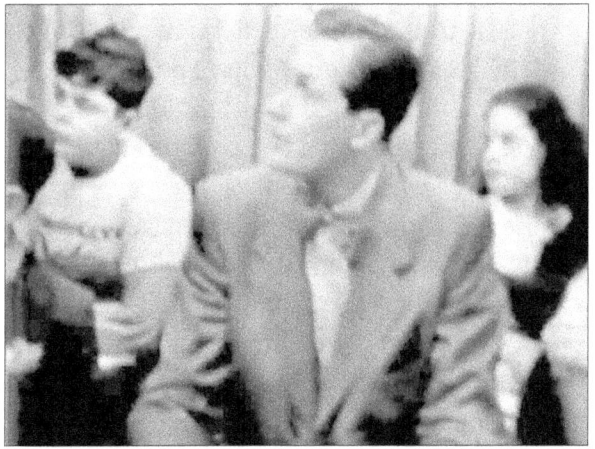 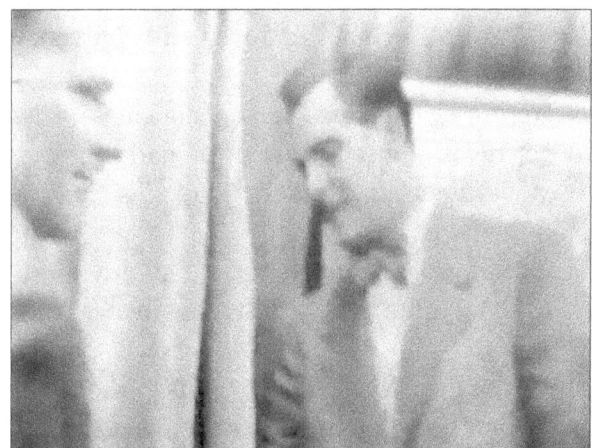

Chuck illustrates, as Jack continues the tale, with children attentive to the unfolding artwork. Jack then joins his brother in the Art Gallery.

"We don't know what it's about," Jack says, regarding the story, "because Hezzie and Chuck keep it a secret all the time."

"Well, the secret's out of the can now," Chuck says, gesturing at an illustration of Hezekiah jumping out of a can beside a creature. "As you can see, it's a toad."

Chuck prompts the children to say the name of the toad written at the top of the illustration, "Herkimer," and they comply.

"By golly, that's a funny name, especially for a toad," Jack comments.

As a prelude to "story time," Chuck displays another drawing, this one depicting Herkimer sitting atop a clock.

Jack begins to tell the tale.

"Once upon a time,
In the wide open spaces,
Where the horses wear shoes,
Without any laces,
There lived a little fella',
Who went calmly along,
With hops for steps,
And for song."

Chuck started the series of illustrations drawing a shocked pedestrian who encounters Herkimer hopping in front of him. Subsequent drawings included Herkimer depicted standing beneath a toadstool during a rainstorm, as to not "get his clothes wet."

Herkimer encounters a robin named Bob as he hops along.

The toad runs into his cousin, who informs him he has "warts on his back."

"Said Herkimer's cousin, as in his head a scheme was buzzing," Jack says, then changing his voice in characterization, "look at those warts, leapin' jeeples, you must have touched some warty people."

His cousin informs him the only way to rid himself of the "warts" is to bury a black cat.

Believing the fable, Herkimer, with shovel in hand, continues on his way and encounters a black cat. He stalks the feline night and day. The cat becomes annoyed and confronts the toad.

Herkimer explains that his cousin said in order to rid himself of warts he had to "bury a cat." The cat informs the toad it is a myth and the two part ways.

A stork arrives on the scene and grabs the toad by its hind legs with its long beak. Herkimer frees himself with the shovel, prying loose the grip, then escapes to his home.

"When he got home and sat down at dusk, I trust a lesson I very well learned," Jack continued, "and with its' moral, I'm very concerned. I'll tell all my friends, yes, even the birds, the wisdom of the following words. When you shop for happiness, sisters, and brothers, don't try to buy it, with the misfortune of others."

Completing a dozen or more illustrations, Jack concludes art for the story.

"Poor Herkimer," Jack says, "he never should have listened to that advice his cousin the frog gave him, because it only got him into trouble. Isn't that right, Chuck?"

The camera goes back to Chuck, standing by an illustration of Hezekiah, with a caption.

"Hezzies says, 'You can't get warts from touching a toad,'" Chuck says, turning the page to another drawing. "Or, lose them by burying a cat." He then flips to the next drawing. "And to say you can gain by cheating a friend." A final drawing is displayed. "Is talking through your hat."

Jack acknowledges the moral.

"I guess you're right, Hezzie," Jack comments. "You can't gain anything by cheating your friends."

Chuck then creates an outdoor camping illustration, reminding always to extinguish campfires.

Jack introduces the next segment, "Chuck and Jack's Art Gallery," where selected viewer illustrations mailed in are put on display.

"Yes, kids, we have a lot of fine drawings sent in this week," Chuck says after a curtain is opened showing the first illustration. Virtually all of the submitted drawings are renderings of the story time character on last week's program, Mr. Buttsem the Billy Goat. Many of the pictures also include Hezekiah, and a couple include Ric and Rac the Runaway Roller Skates.

Chuck and Jack go through over a dozen illustrations, naming the artists. They range in ages 7-12 years old, and are submitted from such locations as Cleveland, Ohio, Michigan City, Indiana, Atlanta, Georgia and Washington, D.C.

Next, the "Artist of the Week" is announced, while Chuck displays a drawing of Hezekiah waving beneath a large "congratulations" banner.

"The *Cartoon TeleTales* drawing kit, for Artist of the Week, and the Cartooner Sets for the other winners, will reach you in a few days," Jack explains.

The drawing instruction segment follows, with Chuck showing the children in the Cartooner's Corner, and the kids at home, how

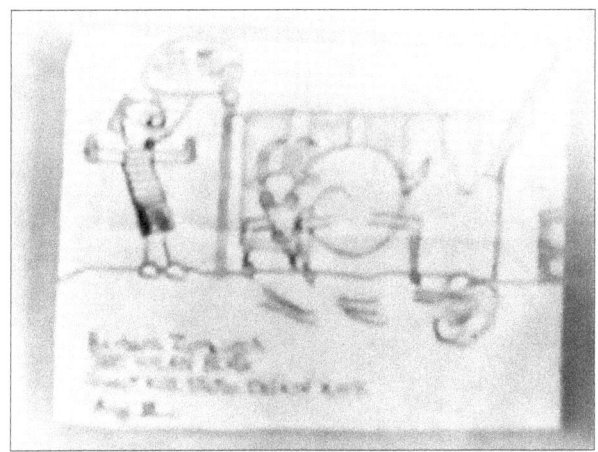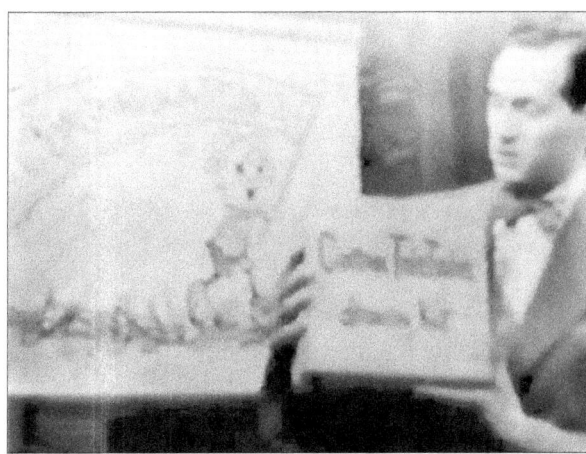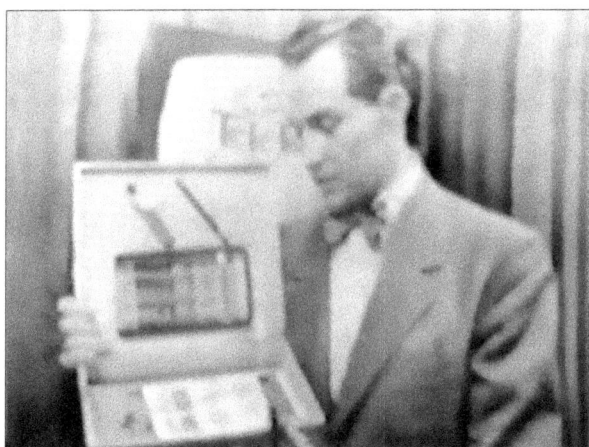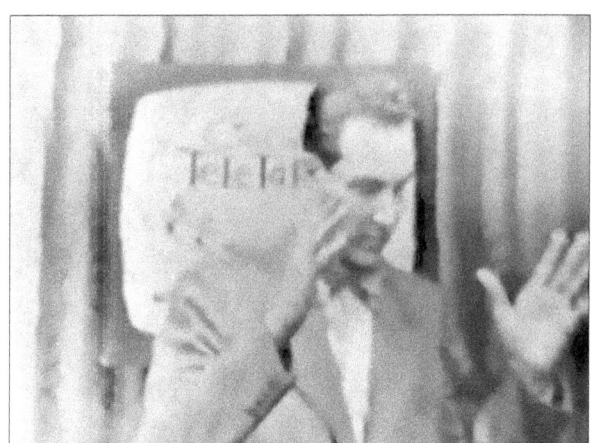

Cartoons mailed in is displayed in the Art Gallery. Jack them shows the prizes awarded, and tells kids to get ready for the art lesson.

to create this episode's story time character, Herkimer the Toad. Chuck tells the Corner kids to get out their papers and pencils, and Jack reminds the kids at home to prepare, as well.

Chuck Luchsinger quips, "To get things hopping, we'll start with a couple of large circles here."

The artist begins the drawing starting with Herkimer's eyeballs. Then he adds a series of curves that make up the toad's torso. Next, Chuck draws the creature's legs, arms, and toes.

While Luchsinger illustrates the story time quickly, he shifts into low gear for the art lesson, so no one pictured drawing in the

Cartooner's Corner, or viewers at home, have difficulty keeping up.

As amusing as the whimsical toad emerging via paper and pencil are the children's expressions on the set. The attention of the young art students is sharply focused, and their faces display both fascination and excitement.

Chuck adds a shovel to the picture, gripped in the frog's hands. He then reminds the kids to dot Herkimer's back with some warts.

Finishing the illustration, Chuck instructs the moppets to add a big shadow beneath the toad to add dimension, and motion lines to indicate Herkimer is hopping. Paw prints are scribbled in on the ground in front of the

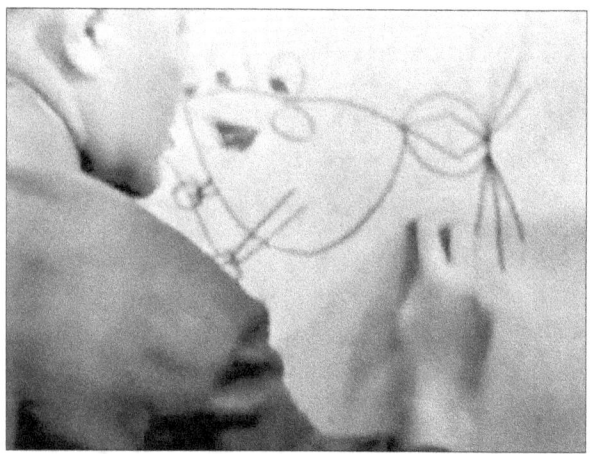 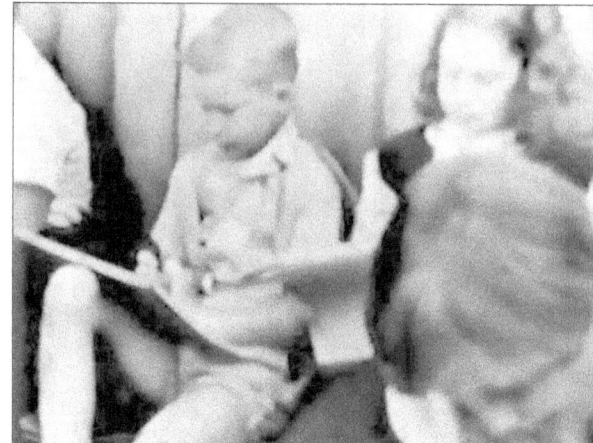
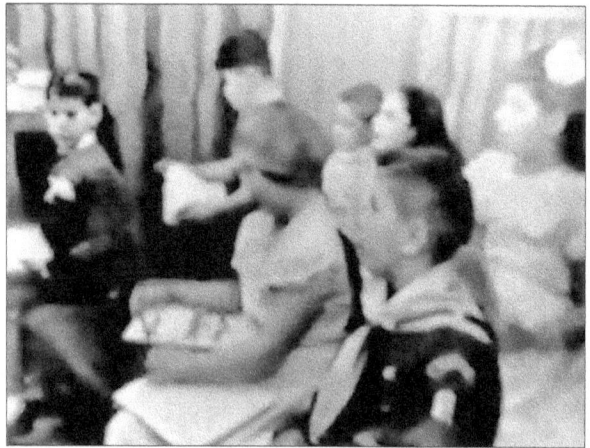 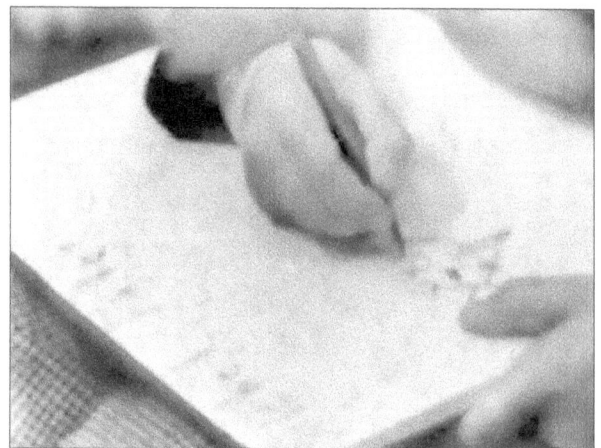

Chuck Luchsinger illustrates Herkimer the Toad as children in the Cartooner's Corner draw along.

toad, to represent the tracks of the black cat Herkimer stalked in the story.

Once the lesson concludes, Jack prompts the kids to show their works.

"Now, let's take a look at some of the results," Jack says. "How about all you kids in the Cartooner's Corner hold your drawings up so we can take a look at them? That's it. There you are, Chuck."

As close-ups of pictures fill the screen, Chuck announces the name of each artist, which is written at the top of their drawing. He offers encouraging comments to them.

"Martin Herman has a very nice toad," Chuck says.

Jack then approaches the camera and points a finger into it, addressing the young viewers at home.

"So, how about holding your drawings up, kids?" Jack asks kids watching the show.

Then he does something that seems amazing and fantastic.

"Hey, look at the big shovel Joel Reuben gave his toad," Chuck says, as if he can see Reuben holding up his drawing.

The illusion is created by Jack reading a cue card positioned under the camera. It contains the names of children who submitted drawings to the show that week, but their work failed inclusion in the Art Gallery. Knowing that kids would be watching to see if their entry is displayed, the effect leaves

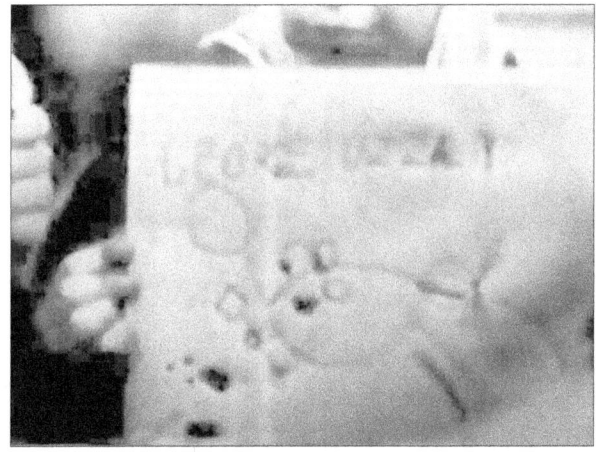 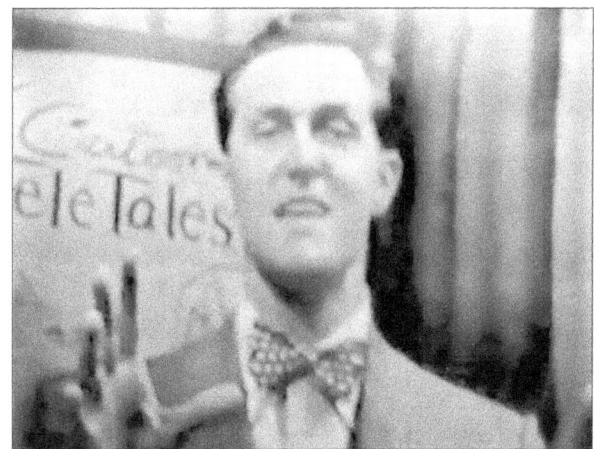
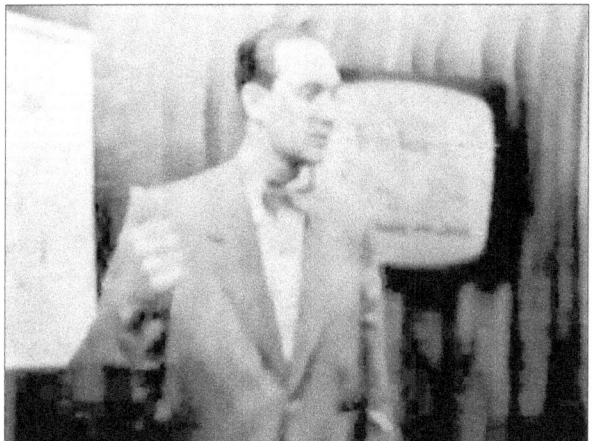 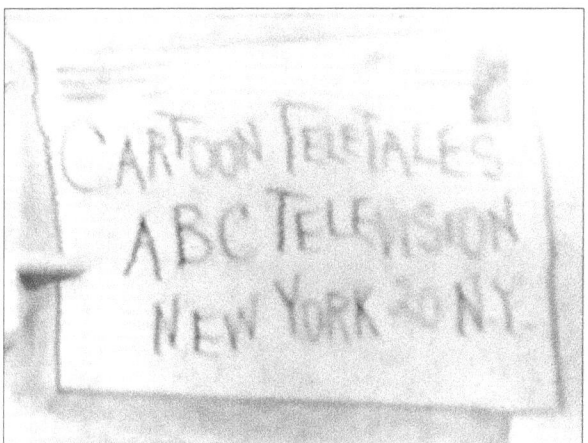

The camera closes in as the children as they show their work. Jack reminds kids at home to mail in their drawings, giving the address.

children baffled.

Jack Luchsinger appeared to be able to see the viewers and their art through the television screen.

Jack then instructs children how they can submit their drawings to *Cartoon TeleTales*, and the address appears on the screen. Young artists are asked to place their name, address, and age at the top of their drawings. He explains that his brother, Chuck, is in charge of selecting the winners.

Jack displays the prizes-winning entries that are awarded. He shows the first place prize, a *Cartoon TeleTales* drawing kit. The large, wooden box, contains three 9x12 inch drawing pads, special pencils bearing the *Cartoon TeleTales* logo, a colorful box of crayons, and a "fun book."

The secondary prize is shown, a "Cartooner's Set," which is basically a spiral notebook containing paper and pencils.

The brothers then present a segment featuring good habits. Jack describes this as Chuck turns out a series of illustrations. The topic is: "Eating right gives you energy and helps you to play right." One drawing depicts a girl playing hopscotch.

The program then goes into its final spot, where Chuck explains a series of drawings featuring Hezekiah, offering a clue as to what the star story time character will be.

The hint is also written at the top of a

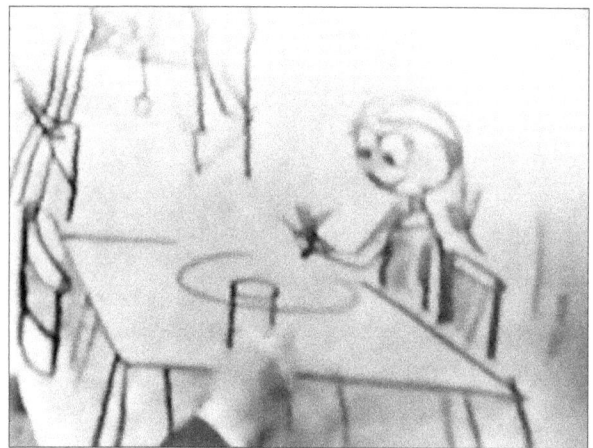 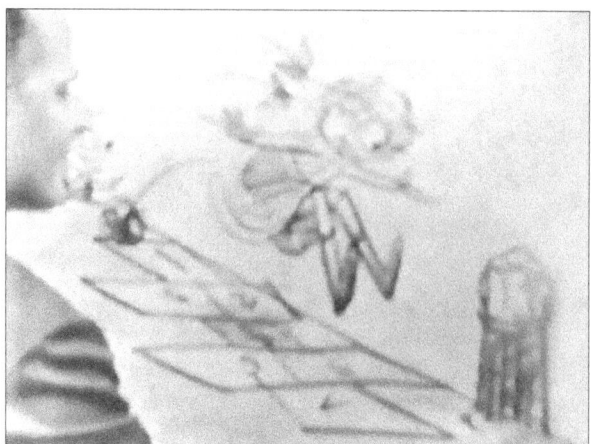

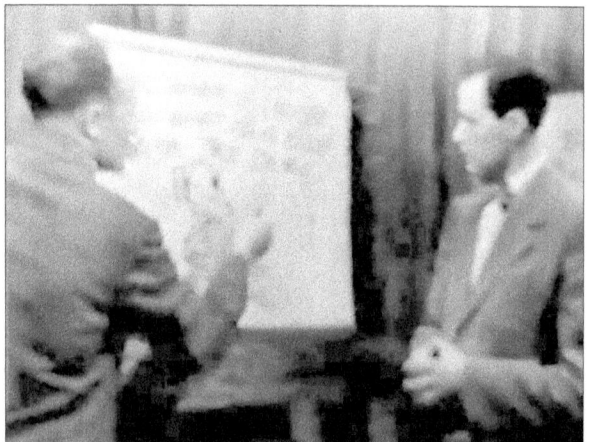 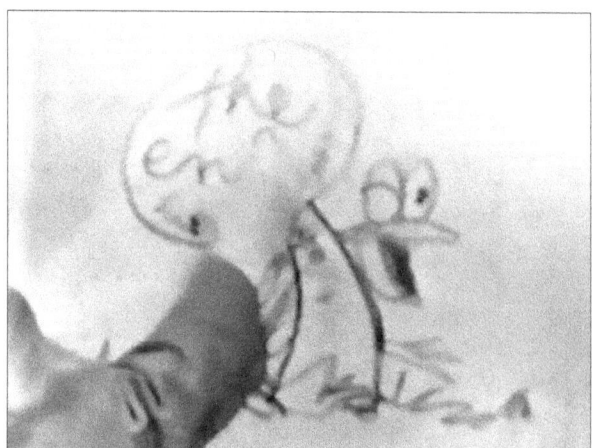

Chuck draws a quick lesson how good nutrition gives you energy, then offers a final drawing of Herkimer as the show signs off.

drawing Chuck has created featuring show mascot, Hezekiah.

"His name is 'Chi Chi,' and what he is begins with the same," the clue reads.

Children submitting pictures of Herkimer are encouraged to write their guess, of what next week's character will be, on the back of their illustration (Kids who submitted a guess that Chi Chi is the name of a Chihuahua dog were pleasantly surprised that they made a correct guess.).

Jack then winds up the program.

"It was swell having you with us today, kids, and we'll be looking forward to seeing you next week," Jack says, addressing the viewing audience. "And thanks to all of you kids in the Cartooner's Corner for joining us."

Chuck is pictured next to a drawing of Herkimer the Toad on his easel.

"And now," Jack concludes, "let's all join Hezekiah as he says, 'Good night now, and good luck!'"

Chuck then finishes the Herkimer drawing, adding the words "The End" to the top of a toadstool the creature is hiding behind.

End credits begin to appear, including naming Chuck and Jack Luchsinger as writers and producers, packaging of the program by Lee Orgel, and Richard DePew as the program director.

The American Broadcasting logo emerges, ending the episode.

CHAPTER SIX

TeleTales' Revival and Farewell

The end of May 1950, *Cartoon TeleTales* returned to the ABC television network with a new look and the return of children on the set, but in a participatory manner. *Variety* noted the changes in its May 31 edition and welcomed the program back to the airwaves.

But *Variety* expressed concern because another children's program, CBS' *Mr. I. Magination*, aired in the same timeslot.

"After an absence of eight months, *Cartoon TeleTales* has returned to ABC TV, and it's a good break for the youngsters—although the playing against CBS TV's *Mr. I. Magination*, another stanza for the moppets, is unfortunate," *Variety* stated.

Mr. I. Magination, which debuted in 1949 and starred Paul Tripp, enjoyed incredible popularity. The program also featured guests such as young up-and-coming actors Walter Matthau, Richard Boone, Joe Silver and Simon Oakland. Actor Yul Brynner directed the show at times, but never appeared in front of the camera.

Other *Mr. I. Magination* audience attractions included a Ringling Brothers Circus lion tamer, and test pilot Albert Crossfield, the first aviator to fly at twice the speed of sound.

Another disadvantage was that ABC initially scheduled *Cartoon TeleTales* for broadcast on Wednesdays. During the summer run, it eventually recaptured its Sunday evening spot.

Upon the return of *Cartoon TeleTales*, *Variety* noted that the show had maintained its

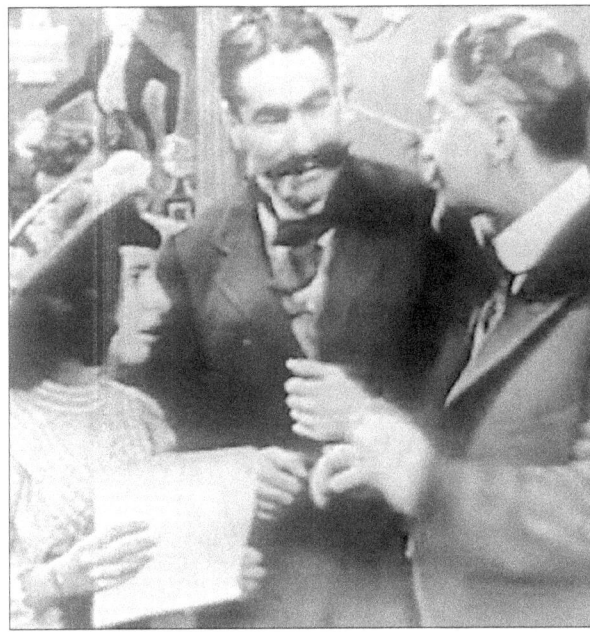

Walter Matthau, center, one of many guests on Mr. I. Magination, starring Paul Tripp.

original, winning formula, but was the same old routine.

"The format of the show is basically the same as the past, Jack Luchsinger reads a story in rhyme (in this instance the adventures of a speckled trout that talks) while his brother Chuck provides a series of running illustrations sketched on a drawing board," *Variety* reported. "The yarn was cute, avoiding blood-and-thunder elements, and had a moral payoff in the advice that 'you can get into trouble by talking out of turn.'"

Variety then praised the new direction for its instructional aspect.

"What lends this airer educational value for the young set is it's giving the kids a chance to participate in the form of a lesson in drawing. Kids were taught how to draw the spieling trout, and judging from the results of toddlers in the studio's Cartooner's Corner, the instructions were good." *Variety* said. "Tots also get a chance to do things, rather than merely to view passively, through a contest on guessing the subject of next week's story from an incomplete picture. Some of the better artwork of the youngsters is shown in an art gallery, and each week a juvenile illustrator gets special recognition."

Variety praised the program as being a show a family unit could enjoy together.

"The Luchsinger brothers handle the show competently, and it's not the kind of juvenile-slanted airer that drives adults from the room," it added.

Cosmetic changes to the program set and the addition of the table (by mid-summer) to the Cartooner's Corner, were not the only changes to the show.

Lee Orgel replaced Barre Shlaes as producer of the program.

Orgel, a pioneer in bringing animation to TV commercials, and who subsequently formed his own production company, Jomar Productions, developed and produced numerous shows including *The New Adventures of the Three Stooges*, and *Abbott and Costello* cartoon series.

Richard (Dick) Depew replaced Babette Henry as program director. Subsequently, Depew became the manager of TV program operations for ABC for a short period.

Gone, too, was organist Rosa Rio, replaced by Jack Ward, to provide the musical backdrop for the program. Ward, whose talent emerged when he began the playing organ in church at the age of nine, was an associate organist at Radio City Music Hall.

With their new team, the Luchsingers

Tele Reviews

CARTOON TELE TALES
With Chuck and Jack Luchsinger
Producer: Lee Orgel
Director: Richard Depew
30 Mins.: Sun., 6:30 p.m.
Sustaining
ABC-TV, from New York

After an absence of eight months, "Cartoon Tele Tales" has returned to ABC-TV, and it's a good break for the youngsters—although the skedding against CBS-TV's "Mr. I. Magination," another stanza for the moppets, is unfortunate.

Format of the show is basically the same as in the past. Jack Luchsinger reads a story in rhyme (in this instance the adventures of a speckled trout that talks) while his brother Chuck provides a series of running illustrations sketched on a drawing board. Yarn was cute, avoiding blood-and-thunder elements, and had a moral payoff in the advice that "you can get into trouble by talking out of turn."

What lends this airer educational value for the young set is its giving the kids a chance to participate, in the form of a lesson in drawing. Kids were taught how to draw the spieling trout, and judging from the results of toddlers in the studio's "Cartoonists Corner" the instructions were good. Tots also get a chance to do things, rather than merely to view passively, through a contest on guessing the subject of next week's story from an incomplete picture. Some of the better artwork of the youngsters is shown in an art gallery and each week one juve illustrator gets special recognition.

The Luchsinger freres handle the show competently, and it's not the kind of juve-slanted airer that drives adults from the room.

Bril.

Variety review of *Cartoon TeleTales*, May 31, 1950.

cranked out stories and illustrations featuring characters such as: Ric and Rac, the Runaway Roller Skates, Mr. Buttsem the Billy Goat, Herkimer the Toad, and Chi Chi, the Chihuahua dog.

While the competition was fierce for sponsors, as the number of children's programs grew, *Cartoon TeleTales* managed to capture advertisers from many sources. Besides being the first network "cartoon" series, the show was the first American television program sponsored by an overseas entity: the Australian manufacturer, Kiwi boot polish company.

The Luchsingers began to look beyond ABC, seeking a larger platform for *Cartoon TeleTales,* to expand the illustrated story time concept. Supporting the notion, the brothers had developed a similar series, titled *Picture Please,* during *TeleTale's* return, registering scripts with the Library of Congress copyright division on July 12.

It is unknown whether *Picture Please* was shopped around by the Luchsinger's representative agent, the William Morris. It appears the show was created to avoid offending ABC by marketing *Cartoon TeleTales* elsewhere while the program will still on the airwaves.

What is known is the prospective program never materialized, and the brothers let *Cartoon TeleTales* lapse into dissolution proceeding its summer run.

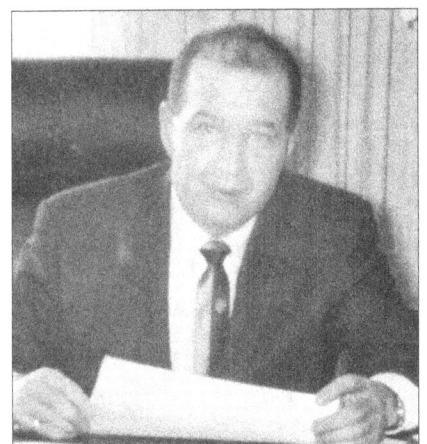

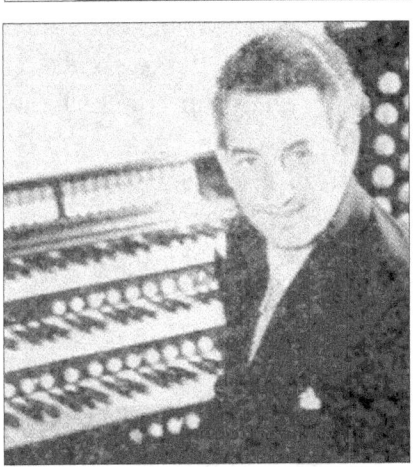

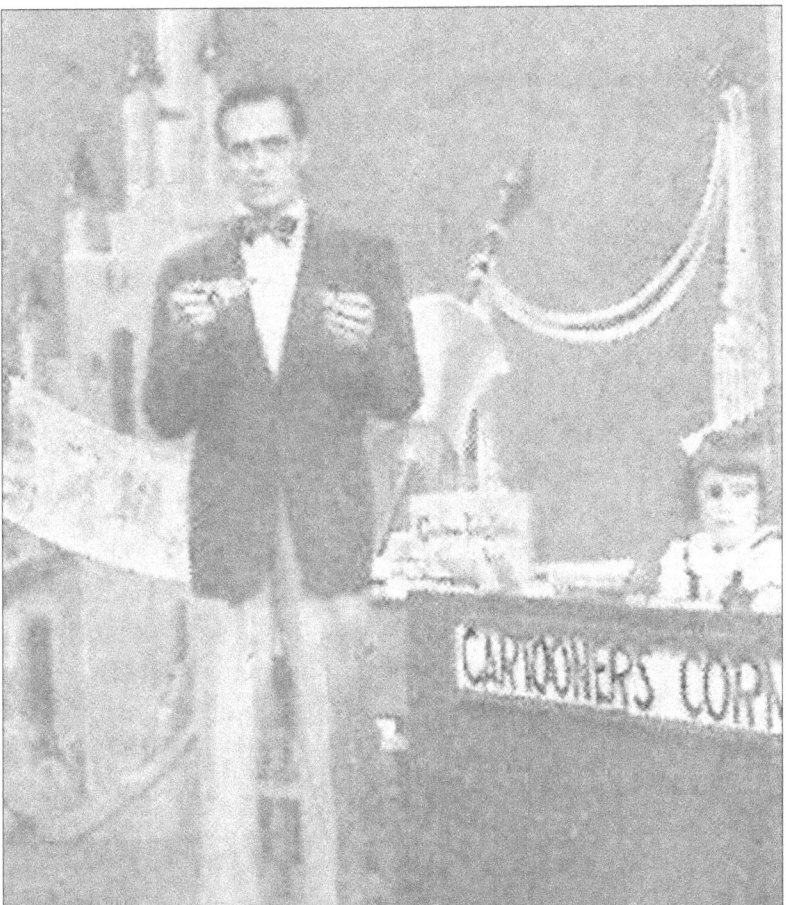

Lee Orgel, top left, program producer, and Jack Ward, bottom left, organist. Jack Luchsinger, right, addresses the viewing audience in the program's comeback in 1950. Children seated at the Cartooner's Corner draw during the show.

The Luchsingers had enough interests, beyond the show, to keep them busy.

Jack Luchsinger, still engaged in theatrical stage, was involved in production work on the sets of several television programs, Bert Park's *Stop the Music* being the most recognizable. Jack also had engaged in some TV acting, his most notable work-to-date appearing in *Robert Montgomery Presents'* "The Phantom Lady" episode, broadcast on April 24.

After only four months returning to the airwaves, *Cartoon TeleTales* saw its final broadcast on September 25, 1950, with the brothers bidding their sizable audience farewell. While ABC wanted to continue the show, they legally couldn't do it without the Luchsingers and permission.

After *Cartoon TeleTales* departed ABC, Chuck Luchsinger connected with Walt Disney, through their mutual representative, the William Morris Agency.

"Walt Disney was kind of starting his [television] ideas, and my father and Walt had a lunch meeting," Bob Luchsinger recalled. "Chuck wanted to bring his characters over to Disney."

But the meeting didn't turn out well.

"I guess Walt Disney just wanted to buy the characters, and leave Chuck out," his son said. "He wasn't interested in the *Cartoon TeleTales*. Walt didn't want to work with him, he just wanted to buy his stuff. So, Chuck was insulted and got upset, so that's when they [he and Jack] went on to doing *Jolly Gene and His Fun Machine*."

Chuck Luchsinger prepared a script for a new children's television program, titled *Jolly Gene and His Fun Machine,* registering it with the copyright division of the Library of Congress in 1950. The script was published as a document prepared for "oral delivery" by the Government Printing Office that year.

Chuck recruited his brother to be a co-producer of the project, and act as a puppeteer and narrator of the program.

Aside from TV, Chuck Luchsinger also witnessed expanded illustration opportunities, and became involved in the development of creative television advertising. He also began tinkering with ideas for toys and games.

Jack Luchsinger continued theatrical work, becoming stage manager of the Broadway comedy play *Second Threshold*, which played at the Morosco Theater in New York, from January 2-April 21, 1951.

The project *Jolly Gene and His Fun Machine*, unlike *Cartoon TeleTales*, was independently owned by Luchsinger, without network ties. This presented a challenge for Chuck Luchsinger, as he would have to shoot and package the show, then syndicate it. The package allowed for larger local television stations to add their own hosts and original content, as a wraparound to the Jolly Gene segments.

The concept was very much like what became Larry Harmon's *Bozo the Clown* franchise, which allowed stations to provide original content within the context of the brand. Harmon, who had purchased the rights to Alan W. Livingston's character, pitched the package to stations four years after Luchsinger's *Jolly Gene* franchise.

The purchase of the *Jolly Gene* package included filmed routines presenting puppet characters Jolly Gene, Yoo Hoo the Cuckoo, and Waldo the Dodo, not to mention the animated segments featuring the *Fun Machine*.

The years 1951-54 would be a very creative period for the Luchsinger brothers, with *Jolly Gene* on the horizon.

CHAPTER SEVEN
Cartoon TeleTales Episode Guide

During its entire run, from 1948-1950, at least 83 episodes of *Cartoon TeleTales* were produced. While the conventional narrative describes each show as presenting a new character, there is some evidence a couple of the Luchsinger brother's creations may have resurfaced for an encore. But, only a couple.

Mostly emerging from the imagination of Chuck Luchsinger, some the characters featured during the duration of the series had clever and amusing names.

"Bum Sniff" was more a description of a disgusting habit dogs engaged in, than a name.

Sippsy, the Mosquito also provided a name and vision of what the insect does draw blood from a victim.

Yakety-Yak, the Pelican, had a name that suited him well, as the birds feature enormous beaked mouths, no doubt enabling more speech.

Usta, the Rooster's name was all about pronunciation: "Oosta, the Roosta."

Lucifer, the Cat, played upon the evil sometimes associated with a black feline, and the bad luck it was said to bring.

Bigstuff, the Elephant, went perfectly with the pachyderm's enormous stature.

Mclody, the Hummingbird, of course, had a harmonic and pleasing voice.

B-36, the Stork, harkened back to the Luchsinger's service during World War II. The B-36 Convair "Peacemaker" was a strategic bomber in the conflict, dropping not babies, but ordinance.

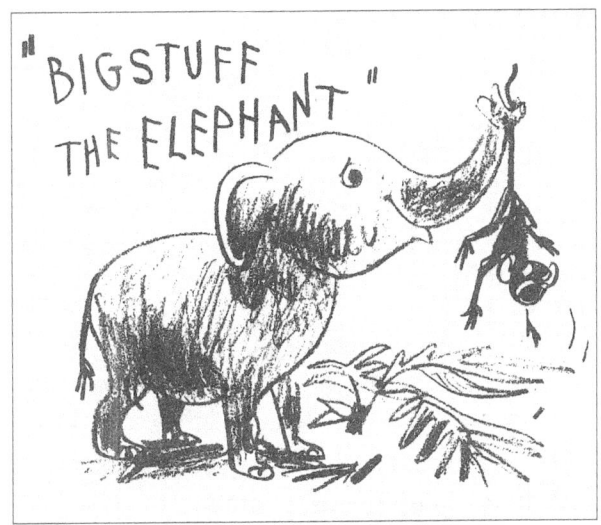

Bigstuff, the Elephant. Illustration from the actual show by Chuck Luchsinger.

Little Slivers, the Porcupine, could give you the equivalent of a sliver in the form of a quill.

Sparky, the Ray Fish, was an electrically charged character that threw off sparks.

Many of the characters in the series had names that rhymed, like Lil' Newt, the Bandicoot and Peewee, the Kiwi.

What follows is an incomplete episode guide of characters and broadcast dates. While records could not be found for every show, the list compiled is approximately 75% complete. It provides a window inside the measure of creativity delivered in the program.

May 29, 1948 telecast - Hezekiah, nicknamed Hezzie.

June 2, 1948 telecast - Rufus, the Rabbit.

June 9, 1948 telecast - Flig, the Frog.

June 15, 1948 telecast - Kornelius, the Kan-

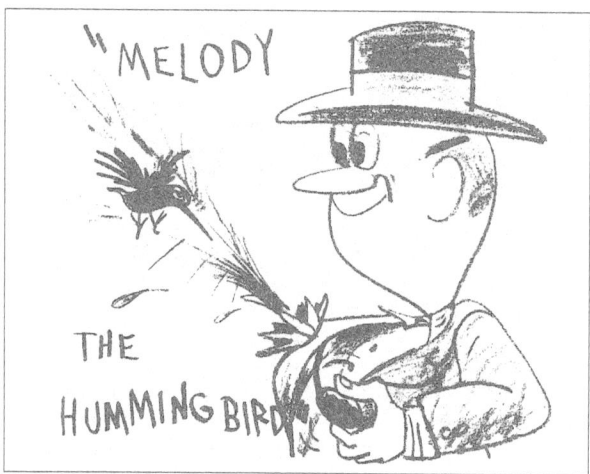

Melody, the Hummingbird. Illustration from the actual show by Chuck Luchsinger.

garoo.

June 30, 1948 telecast - What Am I?

July 5, 1948 telecast - Sizzmo, the Sky Rocket.

July 7, 1948 telecast - Bungle, the Beaver.

July 19, 1948 telecast - Sippsy, the Mosquito.

July 21, 1948 telecast - Maurice, the Mouse.

July 26, 1948 telecast - The Runaway Roller Skates.

July 28, 1948 telecast - Yakety-Yak, the Pelican.

August 2, 1948 telecast - Boo Golly, the Ghost.

August 4, 1948 telecast - Wiley, the Fox.

August 9, 1948 telecast - Hezekiah, the Seahorse.

August 11, 1948 telecast - Hey You, the courageous Lion.

August 15, 1948 telecast - The Adventures of Mr. Chalk.

August 18, 1948 telecast - Feebly, the Flying Fish.

September 1, 1948 telecast - Percy, the Pigeon.

September 8, 1949 telecast - Leon, the Lightning Bug.

September 15, 1948 telecast - Usta, the Rooster.

September 22, 1948 telecast - Mimi, the Mole.

September 29, 1948 telecast - Madcap, the Mountain Goat.

October 6, 1948 telecast - Bumsniff, the Bloodhound.

October 13, 1948 telecast - Geronimo, the Flying Squirrel.

October 21, 1948 telecast - Stick-in-the-Mud, the Duck.

October 28, 1948 telecast - Lucifer, the Cat.

November 7, 1948 telecast - Homer, the Horse.

November 14, 1948 telecast - Bigstuff, the Elephant.

November 21, 1948 telecast - Titus, the Turkey.

November 28, 1948 telecast - Whatchamacallit, the Gnu.

December 5, 1948 telecast - Melody, the Hummingbird.

December 19, 1948 telecast - Maurice, the Mouse and St. Nicholas.

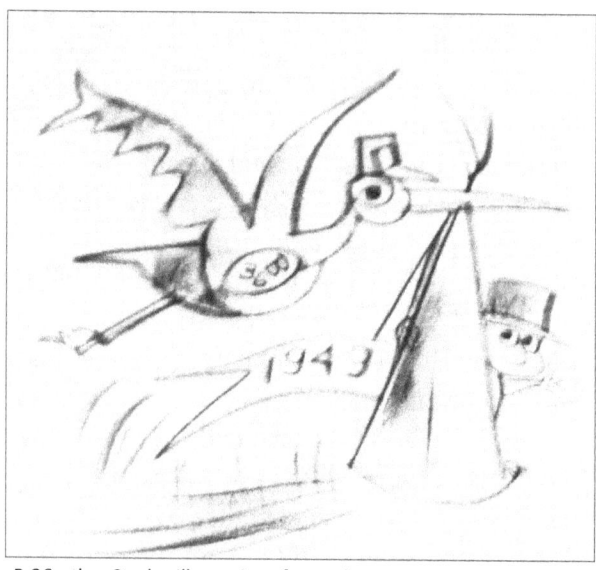

B-36, the Stork. Illustration from the actual show by Chuck Luchsinger.

December 26, 1948 telecast - B-36, the Stork.

January 2, 1949 telecast - Hambone, the Opossum.

January 16, 1949 telecast - Odontold, the Walrus.

January 23, 1949 telecast - Bamboozie, the Ostrich.

January 30, 1949 telecast - Grandpa Jimmy, the Jumping Jerboa.

February 6, 1949 telecast - Gadabout, the Koala Bear.

February 13, 1949 telecast - Herman, the Stupid Cupid.

February 20, 1949 telecast - Torpie, the Tortoise.

February 27, 1949 telecast - Humphrey, the Camel.

March 6, 1949 telecast - Smallfry, the Stickleback.

March 13, 1949 telecast - Peewee, the Kiwi.

March 20, 1949 telecast - Upsie Doozy, the Giraffe.

March 27, 1949 telecast - Corky, the Crocodile.

April 3, 1949 telecast - Roscoe, the Raccoon.

April 10, 1949 telecast - Mozart, the Mocking Bird.

April 17, 1949 telecast - Jake, the Tadpole.

April 24, 1949 telecast - Snookums, the Anteater.

May 1, 1949 telecast - Wee Willie, the Whale.

May 8, 1949 telecast - Lil' Newt, the Bandicoot.

May 15, 1949 telecast - Earnest, the Umbrella Bird.

May 22, 1949 - Sparky, the Ray Fish.

(May 29, 1949 program preempted for Memorial Day broadcasts.)

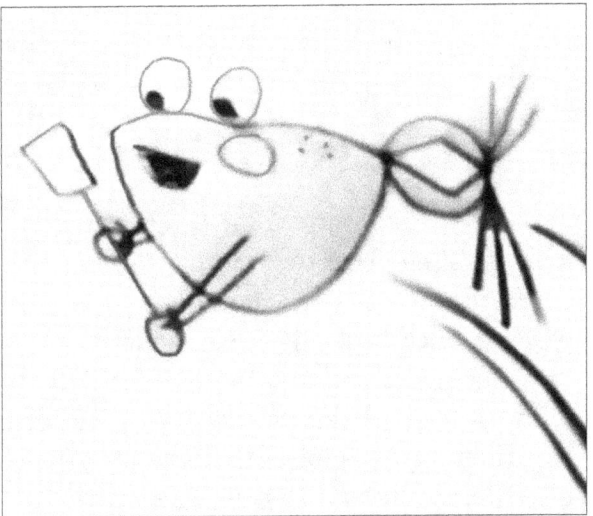

Herkimer, the Toad. Illustration from the actual show by Chuck Luchsinger.

June 5, 1949 telecast - Little Slivers, the Porcupine.

June 12, 1949 telecast - Little Tommy Turnstone.

June 19, 1949 telecast - Panoply, the Bumbershoot.

June 26, 1949 telecast - Scooter, the Worm.

(July 3, 1949 program preempted for Independence Day broadcasts.)

July 10, 1949 telecast - Harem Scarem, the Possum Mouse.

July 17, 1949 telecast - Dipsy, the Dolphin.

July 24, 1949 telecast - Preempted for another program.

July 31, 1949 telecast - Needle-Beak, the Tailor Bird.

August 7, 14, 21, 28, September 4, 11, 18, 25, 1949 telecasts - Information unavailable.

May 31 to September 24, 1950 telecasts - Available information identifies only four out of the 14 episodes broadcasted. Characters presented included: Ric and Rac, the Runaway Roller Skates, Mr. Buttsem, the Billy Goat, Herkimer, the Toad, and Chi Chi, the Chihuahua dog.

CHAPTER EIGHT
The Luchsingers Unveil Jolly Gene

In the summer of 1950, when *Cartoon TeleTales* returned four months to the airwaves, Chuck Luchsinger was tinkering with ideas for a new children's program. With intentions to see it become a reality, he filed copyright applications at the time for a show titled *Jolly Gene and His Fun Machine*.

It would take two years to bring the puppet show, featuring a large, mechanical device adorned with levers and moving gears, into production. Not only was the direction of the show different from *Cartoon TeleTales* creatively, but also as a business model. The plan was to independently produce the show and sell it to networks.

While the program was the brainchild of Chuck, both brothers had learned there was limited financial reward when a network staged and produced a show, allowing them to co-own the venture.

The Luchsingers raised capital to establish their own, little, studio. According to the February 12, 1952 edition of *Sponsor* magazine, the Luchsinger's company was "special effects firm" serving clients in the emerging field of television advertising.

One client was the Admiral Corporation, producer of electronic devices and home appliances. The firm produced stop-motion animation commercials for Admiral, including one showing how many items could fit inside of a refrigerator, and also constructed props.

"It involved Rube Goldbergian props invented by the fertile brain of Charles Luchsinger," *Sponsor* reported. "When Ad-

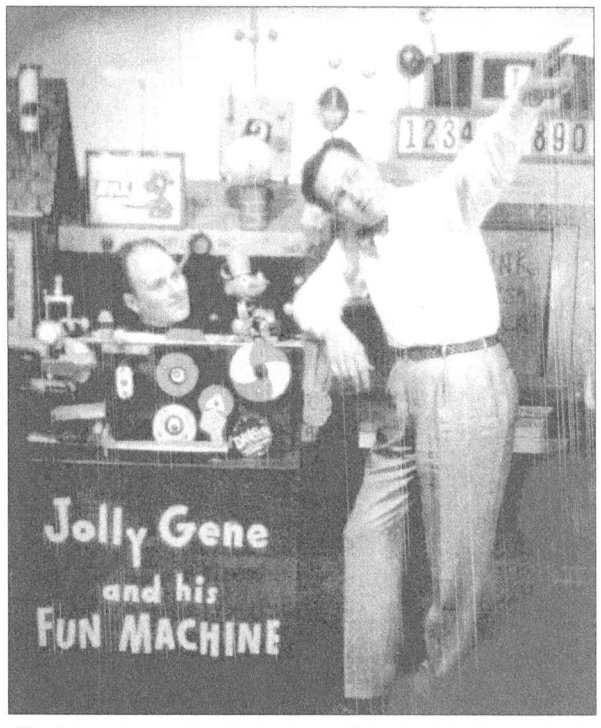

Chuck Luchsinger pokes his head out of the Fun Machine, as broth Jack points off yonder. Jolly Gene and His Fun Machine photo, 1953, courtesy of the Luchsinger family.

miral asked for a replica of its 24-story electric display on Michigan Avenue in Chicago, Luchsinger, for $200, plus cost of materials, promptly devised a production with flares and rockets. It was almost as spectacular as an atom bomb exploding.

According to a September 20, 1950 report published in *Variety*, Luchsinger's association with Charles R. Andrews set the gears into motion for Jolly Gene.

Andrews, one of the organizers of Reddi-Wip food product, entered the television production field with a new corporation specializing in business management, sales promo-

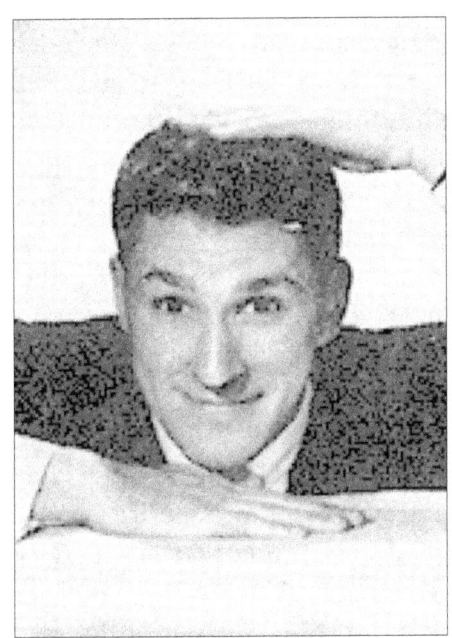 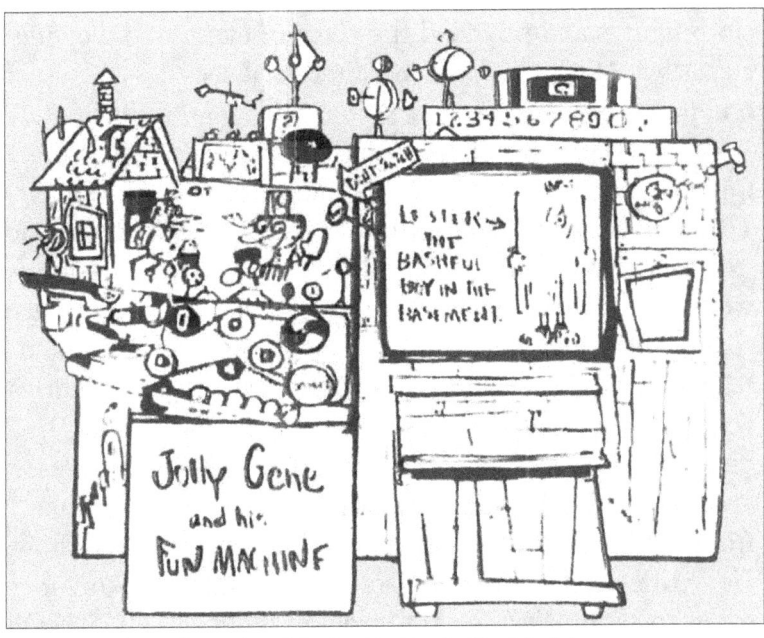

Bill Britten, left, did the voices from *Jolly Gene*. Right, an illustration of the Fun Machine, by Chuck Luchsinger.

tions, exploitation and the packaging of programs which feature merchandising and promotion gimmicks. The newly established company, Charles R. Andrews Affiliates, Inc., represented the Luchsinger's new venture, and the parties entered into a production partnership.

But Chuck Luchsinger wasn't about to repeat the mistake he and his brother had made with ABC concerning *Cartoon TeleTales*. Andrews would receive residuals for his investment in the program, but wouldn't own it.

"The first property [of Andrews Affiliates, Inc.] is *Jolly Gene and His Fun Machine*, created by Chuck Luchsinger, who, with his brother, Jack, had *Cartoon TeleTales* on ABC TV for two seasons," *Variety* reported. "The new airer keeps the drawing feature of *Tele Tales* and stresses the idea that moppets should have a chance of actively participating in the TV show rather than being merely passive spectators."

In 1952, from July 7 to December 30, Chuck Luchsinger filed further copyrights with the Library of Congress for his *Jolly Gene and His Fun Machine* program idea. He also entered the series title under several names, including *Billy Bean and His Fun Machine*.

Luchsinger copyrighted the Fun Machine using an illustration as a guide, and submitted wood and cloth puppets of characters Jolly Gene, Mister Billy Bean, and Yoo Hoo, the Cuckoo, and Waldo the Dodo, both birds. Early the following year, Luchsinger filed a copyright using and illustration depicting the set and props on the show. One entry was "A puppet-like figure standing on a platform between a birdhouse and a TV set." He also followed up copyrighting the show under other titles, such as *Mr. Bean and His Fun Machine* and *Mister Jellybean and His Fun Machine* to discourage copycats.

Besides the Luchsinger brothers, leading up the creative team of *Jolly Gene and His Fun Machine* was Bill Britten, a veteran puppeteer, who assisted with the wood and cloth figures and provided the voice of every character. Mike King was recruited as a second puppeteer.

Subsequently Bitten portrayed *Bozo the Clown* on New York's WPIC-TV, and hosted *The Looney Tunes Show* in 1959.

Britten, with Chuck Luchsinger, also provided illustrations appearing on the magic screen of the Fun Machine.

Alan Riefe was brought aboard as a writer, with Bill Dodson serving as the program's director. Riefe subsequently went on to write a series of fiction novels and wrote stories from DC Comics, most notably, *The Witching Hour* title. Dodson was an established director, who had worked for ABC programming.

Stop-motion animation for the program, involving the mechanics of the Fun Machine, was created by Chuck Luchsinger and Bill Britten. The technique provided the illusion that the gears, belts and pulley laden device was fully operational in the hands of its conductor, Jolly Gene.

Andrews found no buyers in 1952 for the new Luchsinger vehicle. The following year he would score a network, but not at home.

Charles R. Andrews' first sale of *Jolly Gene and His Fun Machine* wasn't domestic, but overseas. *Variety* reported in its May 6, 1953 edition, "The BBC will air an American moppet show this June, in *Jolly Gene and His Fun Machine*."

"The show, a direct descendant of the former ABC TV show, *Cartoon TeleTales*, is like-

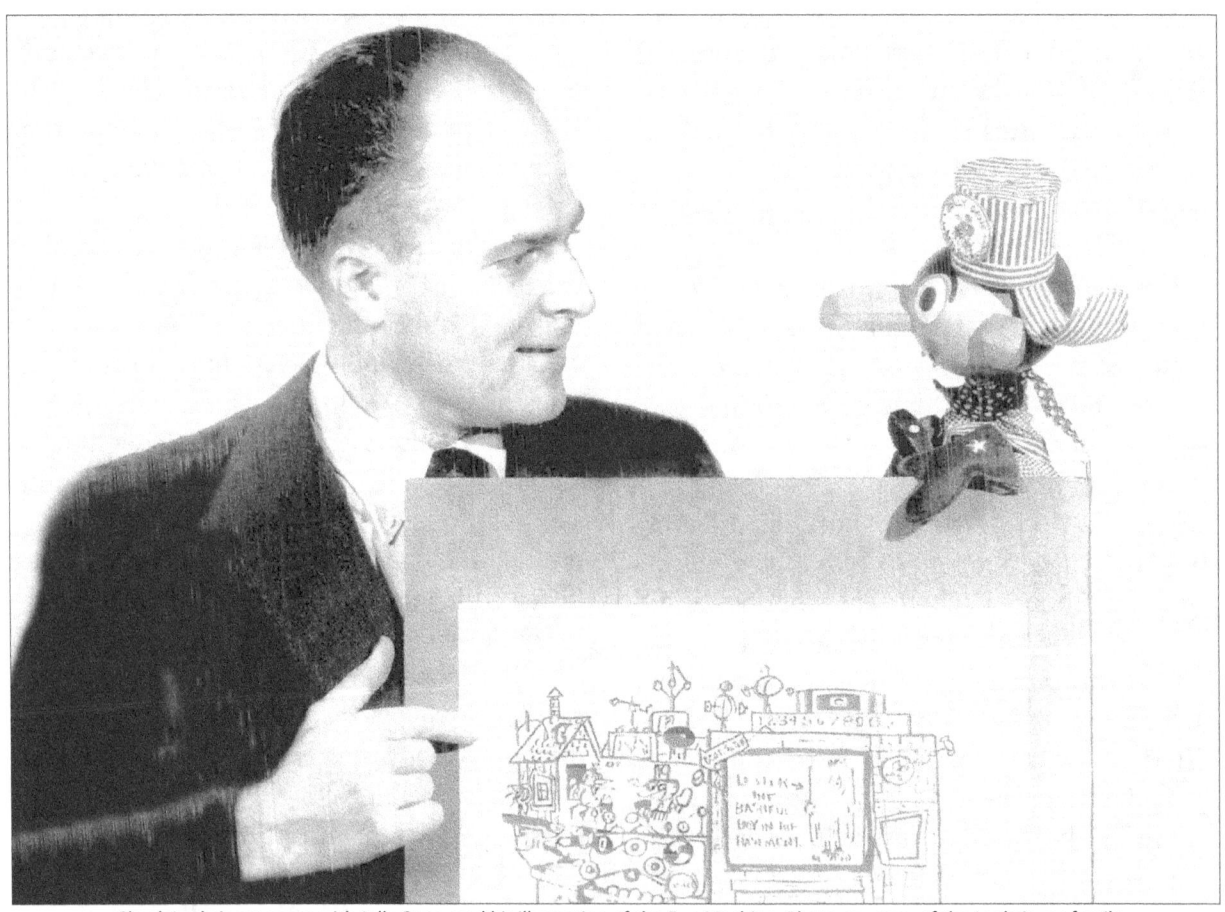

Chuck Luchsinger poses with Jolly Gene, and his illustration of the Fun Machine. Photo courtesy of the Luchsinger family..

wise being scripted, promoted and produced by the brothers Chuck and Jack Luchsinger," *Variety* said.

Radio and Television magazine reported that summer the BBC show would include an original wrap-around the canned 15-minute Luchsinger film segments, hiring its own host and accompanying cast.

Variety pointed out in its July edition while the BBC score was significant, television markets in the United States expressed no interest.

"Charles R. Andrews, New York producer of *Jolly Gene and His Fun Machine*, is in the odd position of having sold his package to the BBC in England, but with no sale in the U.S. yet, despite one year of hard peddling here," *Variety* reported.

The show appeared via the British Broadcasting Company on July 9.

"The show is being staged there by David David Boisseau, one of England's best-known producers of kids shows, who chose it after vetoing all other kids shows he saw on a recent U. S. visit," *Variety* said. "Andrews is flying to Chicago Aug. 1 to talk up the show with a national advertiser who has expressed in it since its BBC premiere."

The British version, retitled *Billy Bean and His Fun Machine*, featured a version of the theme song.

Billy Bean built a machine to see what it could do.

He made it out of sticks and stones, and nuts and bolts and glue.

The motor sang Chuffaty Bang, Rattuta Rattatarator,

And all of a sudden a picture appeared on the funny old cartoonerator

Billy Bean built a machine to see what it would do,

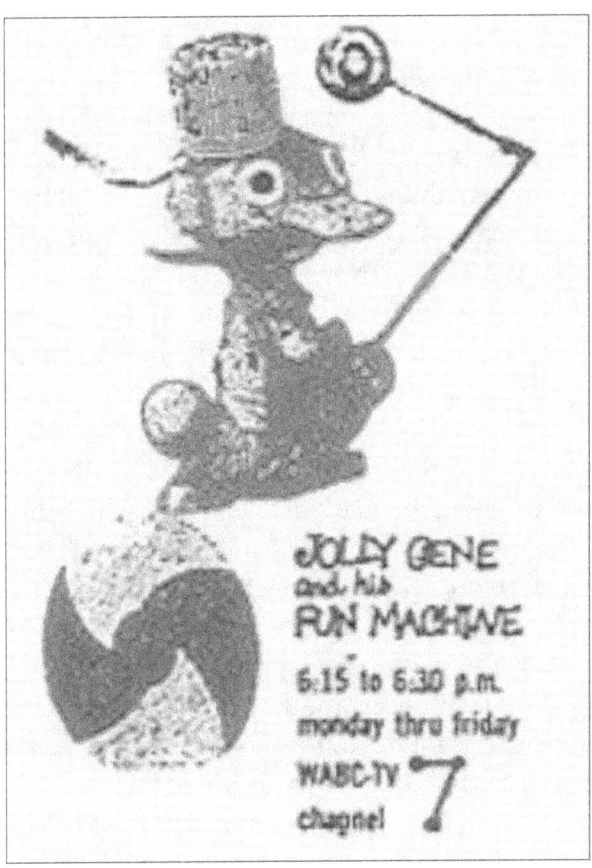

WABC-TV advertisement for *Jolly Gene and His Fun Machine*.

It did the funniest things he'd seen,
So he called it his fun machine, machine,
Billy Bean and his fun machine.

Variety reported on September 2 that *Jolly Gene and His Fun Machine* had secured one domestic station for broadcast.

"Andrews, who was in the unique position of having a program airing on the BBC television network while unable to get it exposed in America, last week set the show with WABC VT New York for a cross-the-board ride," *Variety* said. "The program, *Jolly Gene and His Fun Machine*, a puppet show, will occupy the 6:15-6:30 slot on ABC TV."

With sponsorship predominately courtesy of the Henry Heide Candy Company, Jolly Gene made its debut on WABC TV on September 21.

On September 23, *Variety* published a review of the show, panning it.

"Reportedly a smash video success over England's BBC, *Jolly Gene and His Fun Machine* hardly lived up to its advance billing in making its American premiere Monday, via WABC TV, New York," *Variety* wrote. "This 15-minute youngster's program emerged as merely a loose knit show about a puppet character who poses as an engineer. Surrounded by a weird assortment of gadgets, the comic engineer prattles in a silly falsetto about his varied inventions which includes a 'cartoonerator,' among others. This, it developed, was a screen on which a long plug for Heide's Juby Fruit candy first appeared as well as sundry drawings later."

Contributing to the lack luster rating was the show followed the wildly popular children's program, *Rootie Kazootie*.

"*Jolly Gene* will find it tough going among the prekindergarten fraternity unless it attempts a more objective approach," *Variety* concluded. "It was a bad choice to follow *Rootie Kazootie*, a much better marionetter."

This didn't prevent WJZ TV, another New York ABC affiliate, from picking the show up for broadcast and giving it a try.

The show, with its amazing gadgetry, never caught on as well as it should have. And luck wasn't on Chuck Luchsinger's side. He suffered a back injury in December 1954 that required hospitalization.

"Bill Britten is filling in on WABC TV's *Jolly Gene and His Fun Machine* for Chuck Luchsinger, who's in a New York hospital with a slipped disc in his back," *Variety* reported.

By this time, WBC had dropped the show, and it appeared the gig was over.

Puppeteer Mike King was recruited into the *Rootie Kazootie* program. WABC dropped the show.

Jolly Gene continued to operate his Fun Machine on WJZ TV until the show went off the air on Friday, February 25, 1955. Bill Britten went on to become the third host and performer of Channel 7's *Time For Fun,* as Johnny Jellybean.

Billboard magazine announced on March 26, 1955 that *Jolly Gene and His Fun Machine* had "ended after an 18 month run," but that a number of episodes would be filmed to extend its life and reach.

"*Jolly Gene and His Fun* Machine is going to be put on film for syndication purposes by its producer, Charles Andrews Affiliates, Inc.," *Billboard* reported. "Shooting of 13 half hour [shows] will begin in two weeks."

The film package was marketed by Andrews with some success, but no new content would be forthcoming.

The Dispatch, the newspaper from the the brother's birthplace, Moline, Illinois, published an article about Chuck Luchsinger in its July 9, 1955 issue, when he paid a visit to the home of his parents for five days.

"For two years now, a couple of Moline brothers, Charles and Jack Luchsinger, have been doing a television show for children, called *Jolly Gene and His Fun Machine*, and it's still going over big," *The Dispatch* reported. "It's a puppet show, augmented by drawings, with Jack narrating. Now it's being filmed."

The Dispatch explained that the show, originating from New York, was not a network production like *Cartoon TeleTales*, thus had limited viewers on a couple of TV stations out east.

"The show originates in New York, and is not seen here, but several local people have viewed it while in the east," *The Dispatch* said. "Among them are Dr. and Mrs. Harmon Nelson, who happened to see it while in the east some time ago. Like others, they brought back an enthusiastic report on it."

While the locals were excited at the prospect that the 13 episodes put on film for syndication might pop up on a local channel, Chuck and Jack Luchsinger had already completed the work and had moved on. The brothers kept in touch with Andrews for *Jolly Gene* residuals.

Since the debut of *Jolly Gene and His Fun Machine*, Jack Luchsinger's participation in the show had been limited, morphing into the role of just program announcer, allowing him time to exploit other opportunities. His primary interest in stage activity never wavered and he expanded his reach into advertising. One production on film that was derived from a tale he'd written earned him notoriety.

At the time *Jolly Gene* concluded its run, Jack Luchsinger was getting positive press regarding a 14-minute film titled *An Ice Cream Dream*. Based on an original script by Luchsinger, and animated by William McHale, the story revolved around a young schoolboy named Jim, who learns from his teacher how the first "iced cream" appeared in 300 B.C. Prints were distributed to TV stations, and the film enjoyed a commercial trade premiere at the 52nd annual Convention of the International Association of Ice Cream. Luchsinger's work was also recognized in *The Ice Cream Trade Journal*.

Chuck Luchsinger continued to expand his illustration opportunities, and began developing ideas for toys and games for kids. One plush doll manufactured in 1980 revived a character from *Jolly Gene*.

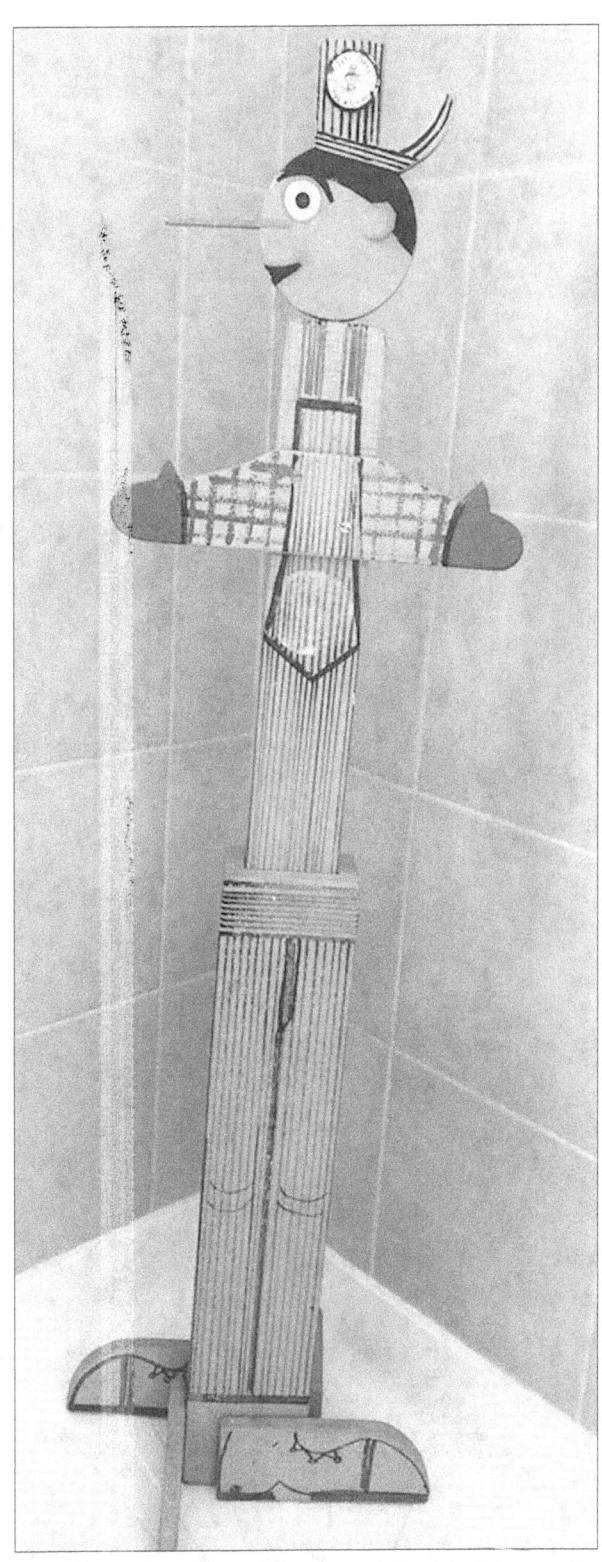

A *Jolly Gene and His Fun Machine* coat rack Chuck Luchsinger made for his children, still treasured today. Photo courtesy of the Luchsinger family.

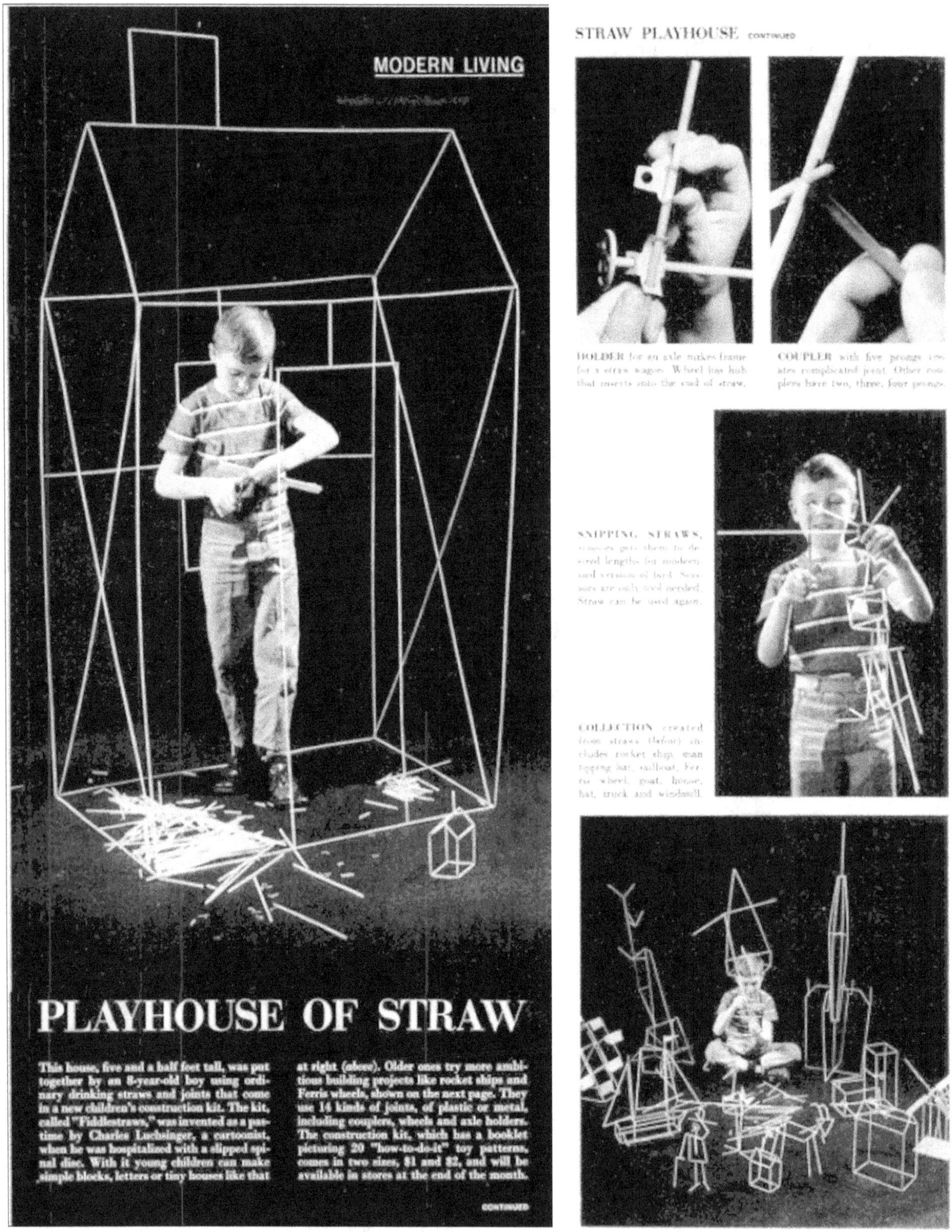

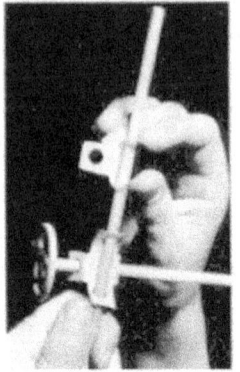
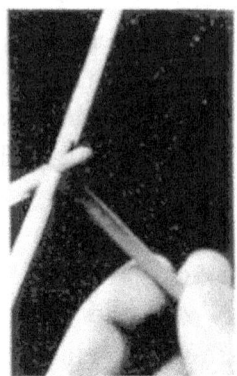
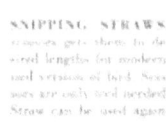
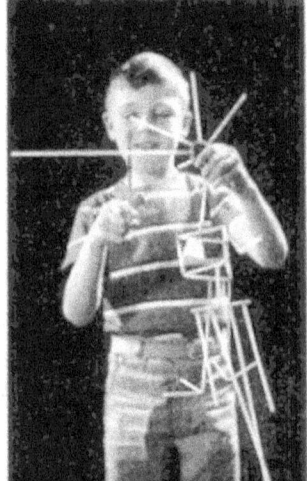
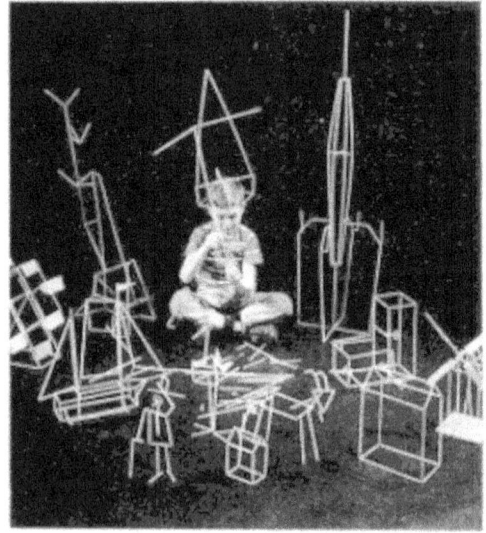

Fiddlestraws spread, published in the July 25, 1956 edition of *Life* magazine.

CHAPTER TEN

Chuck's Toys for Girls and Boys

Chuck Luchsinger fiddled around with toy and game ideas after his television programs vanished from the screen. In fact, one creation had the word fiddle in it—Fiddlestraws.

Fiddlestraws, the genesis of the toy occurred when Luchsinger was hospitalized with a slipped spinal disc in 1956. The construction toy was comprised of plastic straws and came with 14 kinds of joints, plastic or metal, to connect the tubing. The set included couplers, wheels and axle holders.

The boxed toy came with a 20-page "how to do it" booklet showing procedures to create selected structures.

Fiddlestraws came in two different sizes. The small box cost $1. The larger scale straw version carried the price of $2 per box.

Children could cut the straws to desired lengths, depending on project needs. Cut up straws too short to complete a new project? No problem! Purchasing a package of common plastic drinking straws provided replacements.

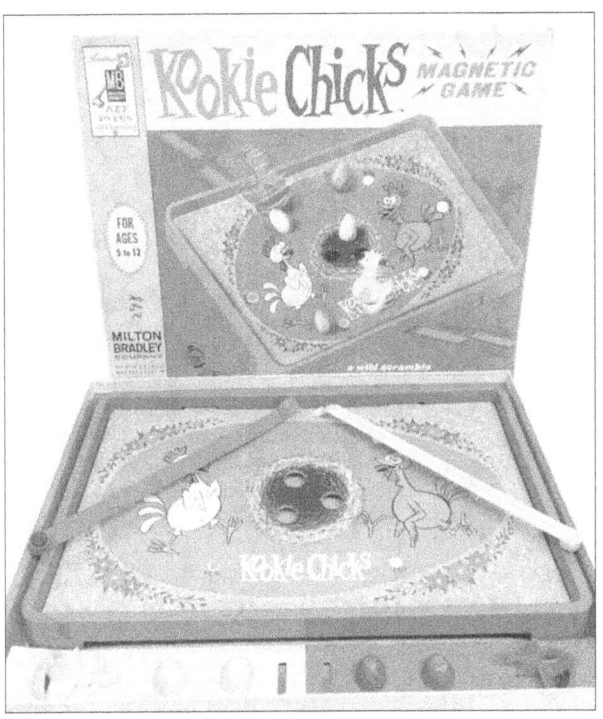

Chuck Luchsinger's Kookie Chicks game, 1964.

Children could make simple blocks, letters, or tiny houses. Adults also enjoyed the toy, and engaged in more laborious efforts, such as constructing rocket ships, sailboats, windmills and Ferris wheels.

The toy was featured in a two-page spread in the July 25, 1956 issue of *Life* magazine.

Chuck Luchsinger's next offering was a board game released by Milton Bradley in 1964, called Kookie Chicks.

The game presented an egg-rolling contest. Each egg contained a piece of metal, that allowed them to be manipulated with a magnetic wand. The difficulty was that the eggs wobbled when they moved.

"Players use magnetic wands to control the

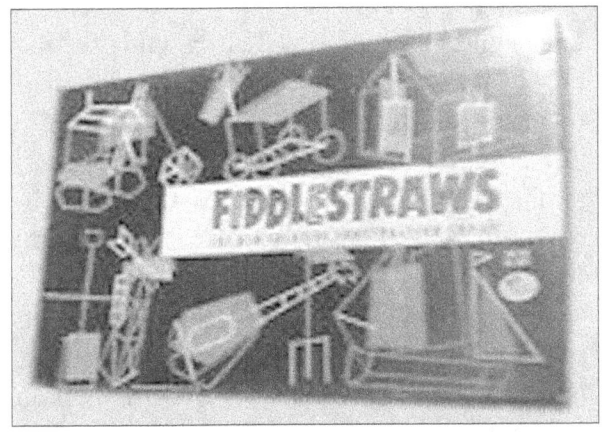

Chuck Luchsinger's Fiddlestraws game, 1956.

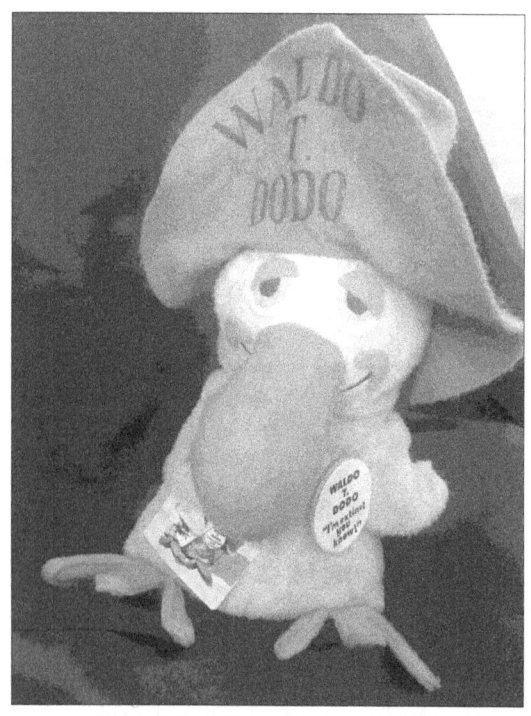

Waldo T. Dodo Bird doll, released in 1980, with text from the accompanying booklet. Photos courtesy the Luchsinger family.

chicks as they bump, roll and knock the eggs into the nest of holes in the center of the platform," Milton Bradley relayed. "Each player has two eggs, but there are only three holes. As much fun to watch as it is to play. Kookie Chicks is hilarious action from beginning to end."

The game targeted kids ages 5-12.

Hardly considered for children, Luchsinger conducted some photography work for Amaretto liqueur.

In 1980, Chuck Luchsinger resurrected a character from *Jolly Gene and His Fun Machine* in the form of a plush doll, Waldo T. Dodo Bird. The toy, manufactured by the Fun World Company of New York, raised awareness concerning creatures near extinction, and carried a "Save the world" branding.

The doll wore a button with his name and the words, "I'm extinct, you know!"

The toy came with an accompanying "Roots" booklet explaining the origins of the Dodo bird, and some advice from Luchsinger.

"As humans, we owe Waldo T. Dodo an apology, and promise to be as protective as possible to our remaining creatures." it read, "especially endangered species of every kind."

OTHER COLLECTIBLES

Aside from toys and games, print items cannot be ignored in the world of Chuck Luchsinger collectibles. This would include the July 25, 1956 issue of *Life* magazine, featuring Fiddlestraws, and the book, *Careers in Cartooning*, written by Lawrence Lariar, published by Dodd, Mead & Company in 1950.

Other books include *Best Cartoons of the Year*, written by Lawrence Lariar, published in 1947, and also *The Saturday Evening Post Cartoon Festival*, published in 1958, both featuring cartoons by Chuck Luchsinger.